LADY IN THE RED
CRANIAL PROSTHESIS

LADY IN THE RED CRANIAL PROSTHESIS

My Journal of Cancer and Faith

by

Tracy McCain

JOURNEYS & MEMOIRS SERIES

QP BOOKS
New Orleans, Louisiana

Published in 2015 by QP Books, an imprint of Quid Pro Books.

ISBN 978-1-61027-327-5 (pbk.)
ISBN 978-1-61027-328-2 (ebk.)

QUID PRO BOOKS
Quid Pro, LLC
5860 Citrus Blvd., Suite D-101
New Orleans, Louisiana 70123
www.quidprobooks.com

qp

Publisher's Cataloging in Publication

McCain, Tracy.
    Lady in the Red Cranial Prosthesis: My Journal of Cancer and
    Faith / Tracy McCain.
        p. cm. — (Journeys & memoirs)
    Includes photographs and images
    ISBN 978-1-61027-327-5 (pbk.)
1. Breast—Cancer—Patients—Diaries. 2. Breast—Cancer—Religious
aspects—Christianity. 3. Christian life. I. Title. II. Series.

RC280.A3.M12 2015   2015765296

Author photograph on back cover inset courtesy of Rafe McCain.

For Rafe, Walker, and Hope

PROLOGUE

One in every eight women will be diagnosed with breast cancer, but no woman ever expects it to happen to them. We go about our lives, knowing that we all die eventually but still believing that we are invincible. Once we become moms, we spend so much time worrying about every little thing that might happen to our children that we forget about our own health.

When I found a lump in my left breast at age 42, with no family history of breast cancer, I wasn't worried. I fully expected it to be a hormonal issue or a cyst at worst. My mom had many lumps removed and biopsied, and none of them had been cancer. I am the youngest of four girls. None of my sisters had ever had an issue.

The lump became noticeable to me in December of 2008. I was so sure it was nothing that I waited to call my gynecologist until the Monday after my kids' school winter break.

My kids were back in school, but my gynecologist was out on maternity leave. Her office staff took it seriously enough to send me to have a mammogram right away. I was told to be prepared to get a sonogram as well. On Thursday morning, the 8th of January, after getting my son off to school and my daughter over to her preschool, I went in for my mammogram. I was completely unprepared for what I would be told.

The mammogram was uneventful. The tech took me in, took the slides, and then told me to wait while she showed them to the doctor. The nurse came back in and informed me that he wanted to do a sonogram. I have had sonograms before because my breasts were dense and hard to read in a mammogram. During those times, the tech was the one who did the sonogram. This day, the doctor came in to do it.

The doctor came in and made a couple of jokes and then got to work on the sonogram. He was very quiet throughout the examination. After a few minutes, he sighed. I knew that was not good. He then began to explain what he was seeing. The lump was very suspicious and he fully expected it to be cancer. He wanted to do a biopsy that afternoon.

I explained to him and the nurse that I needed to find care for my daughter. The nurse led me to the dressing room so that I could retrieve my cell phone from my purse. I called my parents but they were not home. I then called my sister's cell. She did not answer. I called my husband at work. He is a teacher and had his phone turned off, but I left a message with the receptionist in the office. I then called my brother-in-law to see if he could get in touch with my sister. I asked him to call her for me. He could tell that something was wrong. I hung up the phone and began to cry. I was terrified and alone.

After a few minutes, the afternoon's plans fell into place. My sister called me back and assured me that she would meet me at my house. My husband called and agreed to come with me for the biopsy. I made an appointment with the radiologist to come back at 1:00 pm. On my way home, my parents called. They were on their way over.

After a quick lunch, I met my husband at the imaging center for a biopsy. After the procedure, the doctor told us that the results might not be in until next week. He would try to rush it so that we would not worry about it all weekend. But, then he added, he fully expected it to come back as cancer. In fact, if it came back as anything else, he would make them re-do it.

Of course, we would have to wait through the weekend for the results. On the following Monday, I heard from my family physician. The tumor was ductal carcinoma in situ. In situ because, although it had spread to at least one lymph node, it had not spread outside of the milk ducts in the breast.

The week or so that followed was scary. Not because the time was eventful, but just the opposite. We had this horrendous news, but then ... it seemed like nothing else happened. I was given the name of a breast surgeon but it would be two weeks before she could even see me. I can't describe how difficult it was to wait. I experienced existential fear like I had never known. I was convinced that I was dying. I lay awake at night wondering how many months I had left with my husband and two children. I even began to experience symptoms associated with breast cancer in the bones. I was sure it was everywhere.

1

I was born in September of 1966, the youngest of four girls, to Richard and Lola. Growing up in Corpus Christi, Texas, I lived a near-idyllic existence. We were poor, but we had something money couldn't buy, family. I was very close to my older sisters—and considered the three of them along with my mom to be great role models as women and mothers.

My daddy was military and very strict, however, that didn't prevent him from making life fun for his girls. I will always be grateful that for whatever we lacked financially, my parents made up for with the knowledge that they loved being with their children.

I met my husband while we were both in college. I was attracted to his dark, brooding looks and his common sense personality. He is both smart and athletic—a bit of a Renaissance man. We share the same, sometimes dark sense of humor. That sense of humor has seen us through some tough times. We have also grown in Christ together. But that would come later.

We dated for four years before marrying and then another four years before having our first child.

Walker was born in August of 1994. We were both so excited to have a boy. We had big dreams for him, but none of those would come true. Walker was diagnosed with severe autism in 1998.

In the early years, Walker rarely slept. It was typical for him to sleep one hour at a time. We eventually got to where he might sleep 5 hours at a stretch. Then we went through years when he might sleep great (6 or 7 hours per night) for several weeks, and then would have several weeks of waking at 2:00 or 3:00 am and staying awake for 4 or 5 hours. Some nights he would never go back to sleep. I honestly do not know how he did it. Or how *we* did it.

Eventually, he began to stay asleep most nights. Going to school helps. Staying busy helps. But even today, we live in fear of hearing his noises (humming, repeating phrases over and over) coming from his room in the middle of the night. We never know if he will eventually go back to sleep or whether he will start running down the hall, or worse, get upset and hurt himself.

I have no doubt that all of those very stressful, sleepless nights contributed some to my breast cancer. Every study out there has shown that not getting enough sleep is a major contributor to things like weight gain, heart disease, and cancer. And we all know that stress is a killer! While we love our boy, he is definitely a recipe for stress.

Autism has certainly taken its toll on our family. It has been hard on our health, our marriage, our sanity, and our looks. However, God has done some amazing things through autism.

When Walker was diagnosed in 1998, I was not a Christian. I called myself one, but I now know that I was not. I only called myself one because I had grown up in a family that identified as Christian, but I had no idea what it meant to be a Christian. I believed in God, and I had heard of Jesus, but I really didn't understand what His life and death meant to me.

When Walker was diagnosed, I was devastated. And because I believed in God, I was pissed at Him! How could He do this to me? How could He allow this to happen to an innocent little boy who had never sinned in his life?

As little as I knew about God, I knew that I shouldn't sit on my anger with Him. I was angry, and frankly did not want to speak to Him, but something inside me knew that I must. So, one evening, I sat down and had it out with Him. I let Him know how upset I was. I yelled. I screamed. I cried. And I clearly heard his voice. No, there was no burning bush in my living room, and my hair didn't turn white. But I did hear his voice in my head. I will never forget what I heard.

God said to me, "It's okay for you to be angry. You can be angry, but you need to decide, do you want to go through this alone, or do you want to go through it with me?"

At that moment, I decided to go through it with God. I knew the choice was mine, but I also knew I would never make it on my own. I was really going to need God.

I began going alone to the little Presbyterian church near our home where Rafe and I were married. They really couldn't help us with Walker, and Rafe did not want to go to church. At that time, he considered himself to be agnostic. He believed in a creator, but figured that he had simply wound up the clock and let things unfold as they would.

At that little Presbyterian church, I was baptized when I was 32 years old, but I still had a lot of growing to do. In fact, I still do.

In January of 2000, I attended a workshop on teaching communication skills to children with autism in Plano, Texas. At that workshop, the presenter showed video of a North Dallas school district that was using those techniques. I knew without a doubt that I needed to get my son into that school district. When I got home, I told Rafe that I wanted to move. By March, my son and I were there and he was enrolled in school.

While Walker and I moved to Dallas, Rafe stayed behind to finish his school year and get the house ready to rent. He was watching television one evening and, while flipping channels, found a televangelist named Jessie Duplantes. He is from Louisiana and tells funny stories related to Biblical truths. Rafe began to watch and liked hearing Jessie's funny stories. After about a month of watching the program on a regular basis, Rafe got down on his knees in the living room and said yes to Jesus.

Rafe joined Walker and me in Carrollton that summer. What should have been a stressful job search was in fact very easy. Rafe was able to find a new job quickly. There is no doubt in our minds that God was guiding us through that decision and move.

After moving to the Dallas area, I wanted us to find a church where we could attend service together. I scouted out several but didn't have any luck. One day, a paraprofessional in Walker's classroom mentioned to me that her church was starting a Special Needs ministry. The support group would meet twice a month, and they would have someone assigned to each child on Sunday mornings. She invited us to come check it out.

In August of 2001, we attended the support group and church service for the first time. While the church was much bigger than any we were used to, we decided that it was perfect for Walker, and thus, for our family.

Our lives have been forever changed by that decision. Our church family at Bent Tree Bible Fellowship has become so important to our lives. I am convinced that we could have never made it through cancer without that church. Not only that, but I am sure that God knew this long before He put the thought of moving in to my head all those years before.

In 2005, we were blessed with a daughter. We prayed for many years for another child, and expressly for a girl. Hope made her entrance into this world in January 2005. She is exactly who we prayed for and exactly the kind of sister we always wished for Walker. She was only three at the time of my breast cancer diagnosis.

The following journal was written over the course of a year and a half on the CaringBridge website as a way to keep family and friends up to date on my treatment. After the first couple of months, I was surprised at how many of my friends, family, and friends of friends were following it. So many people contacted me to let me know that they were inspired by my words. Some were going through treatment for breast cancer themselves. Others had never had cancer but still identified with what I was experiencing emotionally.

I decided to keep the journal long-term as a memoir for my daughter. I wanted her to know that her mom fought desperately to survive. I pray that she never has to experience anything like it, but I hope that she trusts in the Lord always and that she chooses to laugh in the face of adversity.

The journal entries are not perfect. Most of them were written in a hurry. Some were written with my daughter on my lap or my son making noises in the background. A good number were even written while I was on some pretty powerful pain meds. It has been lightly edited to correct misspelled words and grammatical errors—but mostly remains unchanged in order to capture the true essence of what was happening at the time. Some posts or sections of posts were deleted to maintain privacy for individuals involved. Those were not relevant to the theme of the book anyway.

The journal begins in January, two weeks after my diagnosis, a full month after I found the lump. So much happened that month, and yet time stood still. I was so desperate to get on with the treatment but felt like we would never get started. I finally met with the surgeon on January 19, 2009.

2

Jan 20, 2009 3:34pm

I met with the surgeon yesterday. She is recommending chemo first to kill all of the invasive cancer and shrink the tumor. Then, probably in late spring or early summer, I will have surgery to remove the lump or possibly remove the breast and have reconstruction. I will know a lot more after this week but for now, it looks all positive. Keep praying! I know the Lord is moving mountains!

Jan 22, 2009 10:27pm

I should explain how we got here. About 2 weeks before Christmas, I felt a lump on my left breast. I have lumpy breasts anyway so I am bad about not checking. Something made me check that day. Since these things pop up on occasion and usually go away on their own, I decided to wait a couple of weeks to see if it went away. It did not. Then Christmas came and I got busy. The Monday that we returned to work and kids went back to school (less than 2 weeks after Christmas) I called my gyno to schedule a visit. Well, she is on maternity leave but her staff set up an appointment for me right away at Trinity Imaging. On that Thursday, I had a mammogram, then a sonogram, and then a biopsy.

I knew when the doctor was so quiet during the sonogram that it did not look good. He biopsied the breast and the left auxiliary lymph node since he saw it there as well. It took until Monday to get the results. That was a *long* weekend! And the results — high grade ductal carcinoma in situ and the lymph node was positive as well, which means it is no longer in just the milk ducts and is considered invasive. Terror! I can't tell you how scary that is to hear. So....

First I met with the surgeon. (See journal posting from 1-20-09.) And...

I met with oncologist, Dr. Saez, on Wednesday. I like him. He has 2 physically disabled children so we bonded right away. Here is the plan so far —

On Tuesday, January 27th (Hope's birthday), I will have a port implanted. This will take place at Medical Center of Plano by outpatient surgery. Then on Wednesday, I will have a biopsy on the spot found via MRI on the right breast. It is probably nothing but ... I will also have a PET to make sure the cancer hasn't spread to any other area of my body.

The following week I will have an echo-cardiogram. Then it is back to see the oncologist on 2-9. Hopefully we will begin chemo then but I am not sure. So now I think you know as much as I do. Oh, I believe I am supposed to have chemo for 4 to 6 months and then surgery. Hope has already agreed to help me pick out a wig! :-)

I'll post updates as I get them!

Well, I woke up this morning to add some random thoughts to my journal and to see if anyone had visited the site yet. Wow! 46 visitors already this morning and 6 or 7 encouraging sign-ins to my guestbook. I am feeling loved today!!!

Something hit me the other day that I wanted to write about. About 8 months ago, I was having a real struggle with giving control to others. This may come as a surprise to some of you (I say sarcastically), but I have a bit of a control issue. It is very difficult for me to allow others to handle things for me. And that includes God. At any rate, about 8 months ago, the Lord was really laying on my heart that I needed to let go and give up some control over Walker's care and some of constant search for answers. He wanted me to let others help but more importantly, He wanted me to hand over all of it to Him. One day driving down the street, I heard God's voice say, "If you don't let go, you may be forced to let go." At the time, I remember being frightened by that and thinking," uggghhh! What if I get sick and can't care for Walker? What then? I better do as He is asking. This constant worry may be making me sick."

Last week sometime when I was driving (these moments always happen when I am in the car), it hit me! Oh my goodness! He told me this would happen! He warned me! I, of all people, should know better than to ignore the voice of the Lord! I am hoping I have finally learned my lesson! But then, I am human. Please forgive me, Lord!

Jan 24, 2009 9:04pm

As you can tell, not all of this will contain relevant information. I am also using it as a way for me to just record my thoughts and also to vent. I will try to put all relevant information at the beginning of each post. That way, you can feel free to skip the rest or read if you would like.

Nothing new to report. This cold and dreary weather has really affected my mood today. I am once again feeling scared and unsure. And tired. I just looked at all the messages in my guestbook and it has lifted my mood quite a bit. I am crying now, but with tears of love and joy.

I went to Bath & Body Works yesterday to get some hand lotion that is also antibacterial. This darn, dry North Texas weather is tough on your hands. But I also want to try to avoid getting sick. Anyway, while I was there, I looked over the 75%-off table. I couldn't believe my eyes when I saw hand soap called Cancer Vixen. The label reads something like "created so that every vixen can feel beautiful while she is kicking cancer's butt!" Of course, I bought it! So from now on, I may start referring to myself as the Cancer Vixen! No, scratch that—just Vixen! Okay, maybe not that either. But I do like the sentiment.

Thanks to Angie, the occupational therapist, Walker has learned to open locks. I have had to install a special lock temporarily for the back door while we are waiting to have keypad locks installed. However, I forgot about my bathroom door. He got into my bathroom (we've been leaving the key in the door since he didn't have the motor planning nor the fine motor skills to use it until now) and splattered toothpaste all over the bathroom and my bedroom. He was in there less than 5 minutes, but he is fast.

Hope is looking at pictures of cats on the internet with her dad. She says, "Oh it is so cute. I can hardly adore it!" :-)

Jan 24, 2009 9:26pm

Oh, one new piece of info—I have an appointment ... for a 2nd opinion scheduled for February 2nd. I am happy so far with my doctors, but getting a 2nd opinion seems to be the thing to do (since so many people keep mentioning it). Sometimes the Lord works *not* so mysteriously! :-) So just to recap—

Jan 27th — Port implanted at Medical Center of Plano

Jan 28th — sonogram/biopsy and PET

Feb. 2nd — appt for a 2nd opinion

Feb 3rd — echo-cardiogram

Feb 9th — next appt with the oncologist

3

Jan 27, 2009 8:42pm

My port went in today. It was done via outpatient surgery at Medical Center in Plano. It was pretty uneventful — my anesthesiologist was outstanding! I am in a little pain tonight but not too bad. And I have Vicodin.

I did find out today that I tested positive for the breast cancer gene which would explain why I got it so young and with no other risk factors or family history. Hope has a 50/50 chance of having it as well, so if God is willing, I will be here when she is in her 20s and will advise her to be tested. Then she might be able to take medicine to prevent or will at least know to be diligent about those mammograms. And in 20 years, she may not even need to worry about it. I advise my sisters and nieces to be tested as well. Also, this news leads us more in the direction of having a double mastectomy once I am done with my chemo. I do not want to get this again in 5 years in the other breast.

One cool thing that happened today was that the OR scrub nurse came in to introduce herself to me today. She is also a patient of the breast Surgeon and a breast cancer survivor of 5 years! She told me about a support group at Medical Center Plano.

Another neat thing was that when the anesthesiologist saw my Bible, he said, "I see you have the NIV version but have you ever seen the New Language Version (or something like that)?" He said he really loves his and highly recommended it. In fact, he said his wife keeps taking it because she likes his better. I just love when God puts people right in front of you as if to say, "See, I'm Here!" Our God is so *awesome!*

So, tomorrow, I have the sonogram on the right breast for the 2nd time) and the PET. I hope the weather is not too bad for me to get to the hospital! We are still unsure about what will happen if the kids stay home tomorrow. If Rafe is home as well, it won't be an issue. *But,* if Rafe has to go to work, and if Walker's caregiver can't get over here, I will probably be calling around looking for someone to keep both kids. I hear sleet on the window as I type.

Jan 28, 2009 6:13pm

Today I had the ultrasound and another mammogram and also the PET. I should know the results of the PET in a couple of days. The radiologist found the spot on the right breast via sonogram and mammogram that was mentioned in the MRI. He said it could just be a cyst, but I am supposed to go back for a biopsy soon. Oh boy. I do not look forward to that. I am trying to be a trooper, but I am already tired of being poked. And this is only the beginning. Oh well.

I was quite a sight driving at 8:00am this morning in the ice. Basically, it wasn't like driving but more like skating with a car. But I was able to get to the hospital just fine.

The area of my port is sore and it hurts to raise my arm, but I can stand it. The Vicodin made me sick to my stomach so I think I will avoid that if I can. I even took it with food but should have gone straight to bed. Not really an option around here.

My Power Port, as it is called, comes with its own card. :-) I guess it is like an identification card. It states, "You have the Power!" All day I have been telling Rafe not to mess with me because I have the Power!

I have been the victim of a theft. One of my best friends who lives in Houston (you know who you are!) sent me a care package. I spoke to the post office and they delivered it Monday at 3:15. They left it on my doorstep and apparently someone came by and took it! Can you believe that? Stealing from a lady with cancer!!! I have contacted the Postal Inspector who just took a report. That does me a lot of good!

Funny Hope moment—Hope told us that Christmas is her favorite season! She says she loves to Holibrate! I think she has coined a new term! :-)

Jan 29, 2009 1:22pm

I don't have much time to type now but the echocardiogram was moved up to today at 3:30. Then I may get Herceptin tomorrow and then I will start chemo next week. I'll update more later.

Jan 29, 2009 7:52pm

Here are the specifics—I go for my first dose of Herceptin tomorrow morning at 11:15. Herceptin is a monoclonal antibody therapy that targets the HER2 receptor that is on the surface of the cancer cells. My HER2 markers were just barely positive in both tests. Basically, they are borderline and equivocal. However, Dr. Saez feels that since both the tests run show a positive, it is best to go ahead with this drug. Then starting next week I will get both the Herceptin and the Taxol (chemotherapy drug) every week for 12 weeks. Then I will get another chemo drug every 3 weeks for 4 months (and continue with the Herceptin every week). Once I am done with chemo, I will continue with the Herceptin for another 6 months. Also after chemo, I will start on Tamoxifen which will lower my estrogen levels. I will continue on that for 5 years.

My doctor says that this protocol was developed at MD Anderson hospital and is very effective.

The most exciting news I got today was that my surgeon called to tell me that my PET scan came back. Of course, it showed the cancer on my breast and in 2 lymph nodes but the rest of my body is clean! Praise God!!! Now I can quit worrying about every little ache and pain.

What a day this has been! I got up this morning thinking I had a leisurely day at home with Hope. We were planning on heading up to her preschool at 11:30 to help with a project there. We were dressed and ready to go when the phone rang. It was my doctor's office stating that I was supposed to come in for my first chemo treatment. Did I forget? I explained that no, no one had bothered to tell me that I was supposed to get my first chemo treatment today. I said I could come tomorrow but not today. She said that the doctor will not be in tomorrow and that he needs to speak to me first. Well, that shot fear through me! I rushed over there. It turns out that he just wanted to let me know about the results of the HER2 marker tests (discussed in first paragraph). He likes to start the Herceptin one week before starting the chemo. I then reminded him that my echocardiogram was *not* scheduled until next week. He then stated that he would just start the Herceptin and the chemo at the same time.

On my way out of the office, I stopped by Heart-First (where I was scheduled to have my echo) and asked if there was *any* way they could get me in sooner. I explained that my doctor cannot start chemo until he has that. They said, No they did not have any open spots. Well, on my way home from the doctor's, my cell phone rang. It was the doctor's office stating that Amber from HeartFirst had come running up from downstairs looking for me. It seems that minutes after I left, the person who was supposed to come in at 3:30 today called and canceled. So, I told them I would be there. Yea God!!!

In the meantime, Hope and I went to the store, bought her a toy (mommy guilt for having to rush to the doctors and leave her with a sitter again!), then by Party City, and then to the bakery to order her cake for her birthday party on Saturday. We finished just in time to head over to HeartFirst where we met Rafe. Rafe and Hope headed home while I rushed in for my echocardiogram. Everything looked fine there, so then I went back upstairs to talk to the doctor about getting the Herceptin tomorrow. Phewww!

The Herceptin might make me feel achy like I have the flu. (It takes 90 minutes to administer it.) Then the chemo Taxol might make me nauseas and make my bones ache. (It will take approx 3 hours to get chemo and Herceptin.) He is giving me Tylenol and Benadryl tomorrow with the Herceptin. Then he wrote a script for Phenergan for the nausea. So ... here we go.

On my way home, I was looking at the sand on the roads left over from the ice storm. I remember about a year ago, complaining that they needed to hurry and get that sand cleaned up off of the roads. Now that seems too ridiculous! I mean, who really cares about sand on the roads. Funny how your perspective can change in such a short period of time.

I have done a lot of complaining over the last 11 years since Walker's diagnosis. I have felt really sorry for myself. I can't go anywhere, can't do anything. We really can't even have people over to the house because that overstimulates him and can set off a tantrum. Poor me! Poor me! Then when I got this diagnosis (what just 2 weeks ago?), all I could think was that I want to be here to take care of him. I just want to be here for him. I don't care about traveling. I don't care about having nice things. I just want to be here for my boy and for my baby girl! They need me! What a waste of time that pity party has been. That's not to say I won't have my moments like that once I am well and maybe even in the next year, but at least right now I realize how stupid that is!

Well, I think I will go spend some time with my kids! :-)

Jan 30, 2009 3:37pm

Got the Herceptin today. Used my new port and it worked! Power Port!!! I've got the power! Nothing eventful to report — thank you God! I got Tylenol by pill and then Benadryl through the port (in an IV bag) and then the Herceptin. I was there from 11:15 until 2:00. Next week I'll get the Herceptin and the Taxol.

While I was there I met a woman who did not speak English and her daughter who did. The woman got her first chemo on Monday and then began to feel sick last night. They gave her fluids and some medicine to help with the nausea. I was sitting there reading Psalm 91 which my sister-in-law told me to read every day about 2 weeks ago. Then this morning my sister sent Psalm 91 in an email that had been forwarded by someone else. So, I printed that email out and was reading it when I just found myself turning to the daughter and asking, "Does your mom have a Bible?" She said yes. So I said, "Well, tell her to read Psalm 91 every day. Someone told me to do the same." So then her daughter wrote it down on a piece of paper. I don't know any more than that. Don't know if I'll ever know but I am hoping that will keep her from getting sick next time. :-)

Jan 30, 2009 3:45pm

Okay, I feel a need to clarify. I am not a big believer that doing rituals will somehow cause things to happen. *But*, I do know that reading Psalm 91 and other passages can build our faith to a sufficient amount that we then remember that He is with us and that we should lean on Him. Then HE (not the ritual) can do *anything* and we can have faith that this is *truth!* To quote *VeggieTales*, "God is bigger than the boogey man!" And He is bigger and stronger than cancer.

4

February brought the start of treatment, wig buying, and a new determination to fight for my life. We also learned that being a parent doesn't stop just because you have cancer.

Well, the nurses told me that I could expect to get flu like symptoms from the Herceptin. Or at least to feel like I was coming down with the flu. At about 7:00pm on Friday night (5 hours after leaving the doc's office), I began to get achy, chilled, and crummy feeling all over. Every bone in my body ached. I took Tylenol and went to bed with the heating pad. About 9:30 or 10:00 I began to feel a little better. Then by morning, I felt great again. I've been a little worried that what I experienced wasn't the Herceptin at all and that I would feel its effects later. But so far, that has not happened.

I have a couple of prayer requests: First, Rafe and I have been so busy worrying about whether or not I was going to survive this cancer that we hadn't really stopped to think about the financial ramifications. Well, that worry hit us on Friday. Not only do we have mounting medical bills, but I have taken a break from work as well. While we know that the

Lord has always provided what we needed when we needed it, we can't help but be a little concerned. We will do as we've always done which is trust in the Lord. I just ask that you please pray for financial peace of mind for us at this time (especially for Rafe as he is the one with the weight of this on his shoulders). Second, I am starting to get a little worried about how sick I am going to be through all of this and my ability to keep up with my duties as wife and mom while I'm going through it. (I think it may be all the concerned people telling me I'm going to be sick that's gotten to me.) :-) At any rate, please pray that God surprises everybody by keeping me very healthy and strong through this process and that I can continue to take care of Hope and Walker.

We had a wonderful birthday party for Hope on Saturday and I felt great for it. We just had a few kids here at the house. They absolutely *loved* jumping on the trampoline. We have a net around it and are able to zip them up so that they are safe. It was a beautiful, warm, sunny day. Hope had a great time!!! Walker was even a good boy. He was able to stick around for a time being and then my dad took him for a ride in the car when it got to be too much! We are so grateful to those who spent their Saturday with us celebrating Hope's birthday.

I had about 3 hours of *no* sleep last night. It finally occurred to me that this cancer changes me forever. Autism has done the same in my life, but I'm used to that change by now. This cancer thing is totally new and I don't mind telling you—*I don't like it!* But at the same time, I am having a hard time feeling bitter right now. For some reason I think I should be bitter. I mean, come on, I'm already dealing with autism. Shouldn't that be enough? But then I look around at all of my blessings. I keep thinking, "Yes, it's really not fair that I have to go through this." But, it's not fair that Walker can't tell us when he feels bad. It's not fair that there are children sitting in orphanages in Rwanda right now. (Bent Tree people know the inside story on that.) And it's really not fair that some people will never answer God when He calls.

I think Rafe is going to go with me on Wednesday when I go for my first Chemo. I'm still not sure whether that is a good thing or not. While I love Rafe dearly, he is not the most sympathetic person in the world. He has already said he is going to bring papers to grade. Oh boy! I might be better off with a book. :-)

Feb 2, 2009 9:03pm

I saw Dr. Perez at the Comprehensive Patient Center for a 2nd opinion today. His recommendation was a little different than Dr. Saez but not on anything major.

First, he recommended another test to detect whether my tumor is Her2 positive or not. Her2 is a growth-promoting protein. The 2 previous tests which were stains concluded that mine was just barely considered positive. This other test should tell us conclusively whether it is or isn't. What difference does it make? Well, Dr. Saez has started me on a weekly regimen of Herceptin which is an antibody to the Her2. I will have to be on this for an entire year. The Herceptin can be hard on the heart. If I need it, then I need it, but if the new test shows that my tumor is *not* Her2 positive, then it would be better to avoid the Herceptin. So ... I asked Dr. Perez to go ahead and run this other test. They will use the same material from the first biopsy to run the test (so no new needle for me). Then I will take the results over to Dr. Saez.

Dr. Perez did recommend that I have chemo first, however, his protocol does not sound nearly as aggressive as Dr. Saez. Dr. Perez said he would do several rounds of chemo (done every 3 weeks) and then send me to Dr. Anglin for surgery. Dr. Saez wants to do all of the chemo first. Taxol every week for 12 weeks. Then FAC every 3 weeks for 4 months. Herceptin every week for 1 year. Tamoxifen (hormone therapy) for 5 years. And also some kind of shot that will artificially induce menopause *or* more likely, I will have my ovaries removed so that I just don't have to worry about it anymore. Either doctor, double mastectomy.

Dr. Saez told me that his protocol came from MD Anderson. I know he is telling me the truth as I have been reading a journal written on this site by a friend. She is going to MD Anderson for treatment. Her treatment plan is the same as mine. So ... I believe I will stay with Dr. Saez.

I also feel much better reading that this friend (the woman with the journal) has stated that the Taxol has not been too hard on her *but* has shrunk her tumor significantly! Of course, every person is different and every cancer is different but now I know exactly what to pray for!!! :-)

When I was leaving the doctor's office, Walker's teacher called me to say that Walker did not want any edible reinforcers during work time (*very unusual for Walker*) and that he was running a slight fever. I knew he was probably coming down with a cold but.... He has a doctor's appointment tomorrow morning. Hope has just gotten over a cold and bronchitis, so I am hoping that is all Walker has (the cold, I mean). When he got home from school, he immediately demanded Cheetos and he ate all of his dinner at dinnertime. Also, he has not run a fever since he's been home. He does have a runny nose and his glands are swollen. I am pretty sure he has a sore throat. *But,* he is currently running around and jumping on his poor dad's back. (He doesn't realize he is now as big as me!) So, he is feeling okay at the moment. Please pray that he simply has a cold!!! (And *not* strep or something.)

Tomorrow night, Randy and Kirby from church have graciously agreed to come over to stay with Walker while Rafe and I go out to dinner sans kiddos. Cindy C. is going to keep Hope for us. So, we are going to use the Salt Grass gift card generously given to us by Rafe's colleagues. I am excited!!! I am going to pig out because after Wednesday, who knows what my appetite will be like!

Love to all!!!

Feb 3, 2009 9:57pm

Thank you to Mr. Kirby and Mr. Randy for watching Walker for us and to Mr. Rory and Mrs. Cindy for watching Hope while we went out to dinner. We really enjoyed our night out!!!

We have gotten so many wonderful emails, cards, phone calls, meals, and gifts and, I'm afraid, I haven't had a chance to send thank you cards or return phone calls or even reply to all emails. If you have emailed me or posted a message in my guestbook and I haven't replied back yet, please know that I appreciate your thoughts and prayers and love you very much!!! I will try to get around to returning every email and phone call as soon as things calm down around here a little.

I start chemo tomorrow. Rafe asked me tonight if I am nervous. Well, since I really have no choice, there is no sense in being nervous. I'm sure if I allowed myself to sit and ponder on it for very long, I could muster a pretty good case of the nerves. But, I'm good at just putting things out of my mind (some would call it denial). I prefer to think of it as letting God worry about it. I think I'll talk to Him a little about it tonight just the same. And then I'll take a clonazepam!

Feb 4, 2009 7:01pm

Okay, folks, one dose of Taxol down, 11 more to go! Here is the list of meds I got today through my port:

Tylenol (actually orally by pill)

Benadryl

Decadron (a steroid) (These first 3 — T, B, and D — are to prevent aches and inflammation from the Herceptin.)

Tagamet (for indigestion)

Aloxi (for nausea). This works for 5 days, so it

should take me right through the time that I get sick. I hope. Plus, I have a script which I am having filled for Phenergan which helps with nausea.

Herceptin (antibody)

Taxol (chemo drug)

So, that is my weekly cocktail for the next 12 weeks, all mixed with a delicious sodium chloride base. Yum, yum! Actually, the Benadryl makes for a good nap.

The entire procedure took almost 5 hours today. They like to go very slowly the first time to make sure you do not have any reactions to the meds. Next time it should only take about 2 hours. So, if I go in at 9:30, right after dropping Hope off at pre-school, I should be done by noon. I will need some-one to pick me up because of the high dose of Ben-adryl. Then I can come home and get a little nap before Hope gets home. That sounds great to me.

Oh, he also gave me my script for "Cranial prosthe-sis." Non-cancer people might call that a wig! So, I am getting excited about going with my mom and sisters and daughter to help me pick out a new hairstyle. I'm thinking long and blonde!! Barbie style!

I'll let you know how I feel tomorrow.

5

Day 2 after chemo and I'm still standing (and not yet over the toilet). I have had a lot of indigestion (which is why they give the Tagamet in with the other meds). I found my Pepcid AC today and started on it. Along with the GasX as that seems to be another symptom. But otherwise, I feel great. Hope woke me up at 4:00 as she had wet her bed. I got up, changed her bedding and clothes and rocked her for a few minutes before putting her back to bed and me back to my bed. Well, then I couldn't sleep!! They warned me that the steroid could cause this. Plus the indigestion was really bothering me. It was too late to take any Tylenol PM or anything, so I just stared at the ceiling for an hour or two before falling back to sleep until 7:00.

I mentioned on a previous update that I had a package stolen off my front porch. My precious friend, Sheryl, sent me a Prayer blanket made and blessed at a church near her work. After the first one was stolen, she sent me another one and I did receive it. It is much appreciated. What is so great about this story is that the blankets (both the one I received and the one that was stolen) had tags that read "You are covered in prayer. This prayer blan-

33

ket has been prayed over and blessed at Prince of Peace's healing mass. 'Be not afraid for I the Lord am always with you.'" So, when the person who stole that blanket opened up the package, that is the first thing they saw! I love it!!! I hope they are still thinking about what that tag says and will turn to God. I think that first blanket was meant for that person all along!

Feb 7, 2009 8:07pm

Since most people I've talked to have reported that the 3rd or 4th day after each chemo treatment is the hardest, today and tomorrow are the true tests for me. So far, I've experienced a few things I never thought about but was warned about by my nurses. The nurses said most people are either made constipated by the meds or have diarrhea. I won't go into which I'm experiencing but I imagine neither would be fun. But, I have not yet experienced any nausea which is a very good thing.

I have felt puny today—tired, somewhat achy, run down. I took Tylenol and that helped. I'm also suffering along with most of you with this Mountain Cedar pollen that is in the air. The good news is that Spring can't be too far away.

A great event that occurred today is that my sister, my mom, and Hope took me to get a wig. It is *very* different for me. Rafe asked that I go red and he got his wish. I like it. If I must wear a wig, this is a good one. I also got a couple of cute head scarves. My sister has suggested that I also get another wig— one that is short as the one I picked out is long. I don't think I will need it for the next month or so (although you never know) but I wanted to go today while I was still feeling up to looking. Plus, I wanted to have something when I needed it and not have to rush out and get one at the last minute. I also didn't know that I would be able to find one I liked on the first trip. I liked the first one I tried on!

Hope said something funny while we were trying on wigs. I had tried on 4 or 5 and with each one getting feedback from mom, sister, and Hope about how each looked. I was walking around the store looking at some head scarves when Hope came over to me and said, "Momma, I like that wig you have on." The only problem was that it was *my real hair*!! I laughed!!!

Feb 8, 2009 2:46pm

Still feeling good. I have had brief waves of nausea today but nothing lasting too long, and I have had more energy today than yesterday. I ate good at lunch.

Rafe and I got our picture taken today at church. A gentleman who is a photographer lost his wife recently. He said his biggest regret is that he did not have a recent portrait of him and his wife. So, he set up his equipment and took portraits of every couple in the church (who wanted their pictures taken). Not sure how they will turn out as I forgot blush this morning, but oh well.

Funny story — First, for those of you who do not know Walker very well, I should tell you that Walker puts *everything* in his mouth. Once he ate half of a five dollar bill!!! And once he ate half of a lotto ticket. Luckily, it wasn't the winning ticket. Anyway, you will probably see where this story is going pretty quickly. This morning, our Pastor, Pete was talking about God's grace and how many of us may have the gift of God's grace in a neatly wrapped package sitting on our dressers still waiting to be unwrapped. Rafe leaned over to me and said, "Walker ate it!" I laughed so hard I thought they might kick us out of church! Then we got to drawing pictures back and forth of Walker eating this package labeled "God's Grace" and then God saying, "That's okay, Walker, enjoy! There's plenty for everyone!"

Love, love!!!

Feb 8, 2009 7:26pm

A friend has so graciously set up a Care Calendar for us. This is where people who are wondering what they can do for us and how they can pray for us can sign up for meals and rides and other things or just get prayer ideas online. She has wanted to send out this address for a while but I was holding it up until I had a better idea of what days I will feel too sick (or too lazy) to cook and what days I will need someone to pick up Hope, etc. Anyway, we think we have it now. It may change a little as time goes on. Here is that info.

Thank you all so much!!!

Feb 9, 2009 4:43pm

Saw the oncologist today. Just a routine visit. He checked my reflexes. Neuropathy is a common side effect from the Taxol, so he is looking for signs of that. He checked the size of my tumor—no changes *yet*! He also is going to start giving me my iron through my port on my treatment days instead of my having to take it orally. That will help with some other issues I'm having. :-) So, it seems that my first chemo treatment has gone by without any major problems. Phew!

Feb 12, 2009 11:18am

Dear Loved ones,

I had my 2nd chemo infusion yesterday. The only problem that occurred is that I was told it would only take 2 hours but it took 5!!! My friend, Cindy D., took me to the treatment. I felt bad for her because I told her we would be done by 12:30 at the latest. We didn't get out of there until after 2:30. Plus, I had to call my friend Sheila to take Hope home with her and Shane. (Hope was thrilled and didn't want to come home when it was time!).

The only issue I had last night was just being so sleepy from the Benadryl. Then by bedtime, I couldn't sleep because of the steroid. I took a Tylenol PM and that helped but I still woke up frequently.

I saw my friend, Mrs. Lopez, again. She gets her chemo treatments on Wednesday as well. She doesn't speak English, and my Spanish is *very* limited but we try. Her daughter interprets for us when she is in the room. Mrs. Lopez told me yesterday that her hair is falling out. She was there to get her 4th infusion, so I probably have 2 more weeks with hair. Oh boy! At least I have my wig and several hair wraps ready for just such an occasion. I was advised to go and get a really short haircut. It is easier to clean up short hair than long hair.

I have another update on the saga of the missing package. Yesterday morning when I opened the front door to send Walker out to the bus, the package was on the front porch. We had a rainstorm the night before and since the package was not wet, I concluded that whoever left it must have dropped it off that morning. It was unopened. I am guessing that it was accidentally delivered to one of my neighbors and they just kept forgetting to bring it over. I asked my friend, Sheryl, about what to do with the prayer blanket in that package and she agreed that I should hand it on to Mrs. Lopez. I think she will really appreciate it.

I know a lot of people think I am strong but trust me, I am not. I just know that I am not alone. My Lord is always with me. Only He knows the outcome which is both comforting and a little scary at the same time. But I know He loves me and knows what is best for me. He chose *me*! That is not something I take lightly. Plus, I really don't have any choice but to seek treatment. I have 2 kids to raise — one very special boy who needs me and a very amazing girl who needs her mom to teach her about how much God loves her. She was chosen as well. She has a very important purpose on this earth and I want to be the one to help her see that. God blessed me with lots of reasons to fight!

Go out and have a great day!!

Feb 13, 2009 10:13am

I had a headache last night, just like the one I had last Thursday night. I don't think this one was as severe. It has subsided by this morning, thankfully. So, if that is the worst I get from the Taxol cocktail, then I am fine with that. I've also noticed that my vision is not great. Of course, that could be just my 42 year old eyes. I've never worn glasses, so it may be time to head to the eye doctor.

Feb 13, 2009 4:47pm

The doctor said I would get neuropathy in my hands and fingers and yes, that has hit me today. My fingers are numb. I've also had a nosebleed today. Maybe more information than you all wanted to know, but I made the decision to be as honest as possible (and still have a little bit of dignity).

Feb 15, 2009 2:32pm

Feeling okay today. Hands still shaky and numb. I had my puny, just-feeling-kinda-yucky day yesterday. Basically, if I had the kind of life where I could just lay in bed and watch movies all Saturday, it would have been fine. *But* since I don't, well ... I just get up and go on.

Rafe is now on the couch after giving blood this morning at church. He says he is going to use it as an excuse to rest and will now give blood every Sunday!

This morning, Pastor Pete talked about defining moments in life. He described three in his — the day he and his wife were married, the day his first son was born, and the day that he, at age 4, accepted Jesus as his Savior. Of course, I too count the day I married Rafe and the days that my kids were born as defining moments in my life. I have a few others:

The series of days that Walker was tested and diagnosed with autism stand out as days that changed me forever. Walker was 3. I can remember one night in particular during that time after we finally got Walker to sleep, Rafe and I were in our bed in our little house in Corpus Christi, and I laid there in the dark and cried (and screamed) so loud that I was afraid I would wake Walker up. I was so angry, at life, at God, at everything.

More recently, the day I had my mammogram and biopsy and that doctor looked at me and said, "This isn't going to be some little benign thing." That day changed me forever.

Another defining moment for me and also for our family was the night we went into what was then called the Special Needs support group at our church. I walked in there thinking I was going to educate them on Walker, on my family, on autism. Ha!!! I have learned more from our Special Needs family than I could ever imagine! Most importantly, I've grown to love all of them so much. That night was a night that changed me forever.

Another truly life changing experience also happened at church for me, but this one was in a new believers' class I took about 7 years ago. I will never forget the moment! We had been talking about how you cannot earn God's grace and therefore, you can't do anything to keep it nor can you do anything to lose it. Intellectually, I knew that, but for some reason, something someone said that day struck me and suddenly, I got it!!! I sat straight up and said, "Wow! Weird!!!" Everyone looked at me like I had lost it! It wasn't what was said that was weird to me. It was the fact that even though I had heard it before, it finally made sense. Sort of like looking at a 3D art picture. You know, the ones where the image is just a bunch of dots or squiggles. But then, you sit and focus on it for a long time until finally the picture comes into view. But the picture was there all along. You just finally saw it. Only, I didn't do anything to see God's truth. He just finally made it clear to me. That was what seemed weird to me. And also fabulous!!! God's truth is fabulous and the moments that He chooses to reveal that His Truths to us are fabulous, even when they are also painful.

One more note: The song we sang this morning—I have a hope! (And yes, I can't help but think about our little Hope when I sing that song.) But the line that struck me today, "He turns my darkness into light!" Is it just me, or does anyone else see the light here? I hope you can all see it because I definitely see it! And it's very bright!! Where are my sunglasses?

Feb 17, 2009 9:47am

I was just thinking about this darkness that God has turned into light. I see this tumor and this breast and those lymph nodes as the darkness. It's like this evil that is attached to me. *But*, surrounding it on all sides is a light—from my heart because it is filled with God's Holy Spirit and from all the friends and family who have stepped forward to say, "*No*, we will not let this take her! We will pray!!!" God has just turned on a light here! I see it in every person who comes up to me to say they are praying. I see it in my daughter's pediatrician who sent me a personal note to say he is praying for me. I see it in my son's teacher who doesn't send home a note in the afternoon without also saying, "I am praying for you!" And she sends home a lot of notes. I see it in my great Aunt and family in Ohio who have never met me in person but has sent me a Get Well card almost every week. And in her daughter-in-law who posts messages to me regularly and always gives me something to really think about and/or encourage me. And to all those who say, "You don't know me but ... I know your sister, your cousin, your aunt, your friend. And I am praying." This is the true miracle regardless of what happens to me. I suppose that anyone who experiences a life threatening disease sees this same thing, but I am just astonished by it and so I am recording it here. I hope that you all can see it and are amazed by the work of His hands!

Feb 17, 2009 8:52pm

Well, I did it!! I went today and got my hair cut really short. Do I like it? Well, no, not as much as the shoulder length hair that took *sooo* long to grow, but ... I guess this is my way of taking control of an uncontrollable situation. I will lose my hair, but now, it's on *my* terms! I've heard from others that losing your hair is very traumatic. So, I'm hoping that this will ease it just a little. Plus, I think it will be easier to clean up those falling short hairs rather than the long ones. I will try to post pics later.

Tomorrow is my chemo day, so I will be at the Plano Cancer Institute *all* day tomorrow. If you need me, you can reach me there. I'll have my cell phone on me. :-) But, I'll warn you, the Benadryl makes me drunk!

Feb 19, 2009 10:01am

Hi all,

Well, I made it through yesterday's infusion with no issues. I had loads of fun with my good friends, Sara and Jamie yesterday. Both came up, brought gifts and lunch. Jamie has been battling cancer for over 3 1/2 years now, so she brought me a very nice care package of things she wished she had when she first started. It was nice to get to ask Jamie all kinds of questions about this whole experience. And it was very nice to sit and just catch up with both of them. I am discovering that Wednesdays are my relaxing days. I get to sit and let others take care of me for a change.

In case you haven't yet discovered, I have posted some more pictures here. No pics of the short hair yet, but there are some good pics of the kids and one of Rafe and I that was just taken at church. I am so glad we waited in line that morning to get our picture taken.

To my sweet friend, Donna: I don't know about the "strength in Tracy McCain" because I certainly don't feel strong at all. But I do know that Satan completely underestimated the power of the prayers of all of my loved ones. But God knew all along!

Tomorrow I will start to feel the neuropathy. It starts on Friday, continues through the weekend, and then goes away just in time to get another infusion. :-)

Feb 21, 2009 12:02pm

Just when I think I have all of this figured out, the rules change on me. I do not appear to have the neuropathy this week, or if I have it at all, it is not nearly as bad. Could it be because of the glutathione and B12 that my new friend Ronda told me about? I am a little queasy today. My allergies have been driving me crazy and that can contribute to the stomach upset. I did *not* have a headache at all this Thursday but instead had a headache all day Friday. It was clearly a sinus headache. I have given up the Flonase since it can cause nosebleeds, and I'm already suffering from those. I am also a little achy today.

No hair loss yet, but I was afraid to wash my hair this morning but I did it anyway. I am afraid for it to start coming out and yet, I want to go ahead and get it over with. I feel like the hair thing is a big hurdle that I need to get over, even though I dread it.

And while my body is tired and says, "I need rest," my spirit says, "I'm bored!" Those are words Rafe absolutely *dreads* coming from me!

Happy Saturday!

Feb 22, 2009 9:40am

Will have blood work done on Monday. They check it every time I go in for my chemo, but Dr. Saez wants to check it again on Monday. He said my levels are still within the normal range, but he wants to check them again on Monday to see if they have dipped below normal. If they have, they will give me a shot to raise my white blood cell count. They will raise them up just in time to have them knocked down again by Wednesday's chemo.

I see Dr. Saez again on Wednesday after my chemo appt. He will be checking to see if the tumor has decreased in size and also checking for any side effects from the chemo/steroids.

I think I have 'roid rage! I am pretty cranky right now! My poor Rafe! He is getting the brunt of it. If he comes to church with a black eye, please ignore! :-)

I got some Zyrtec yesterday for my allergies. They are a little better this morning. At Walgreens last night, I was standing in line while Rafe was out in the truck with both kids when someone ran past me. I looked up and saw Rafe running in and yelling, "Walker." Walker had jumped out of the front seat of the truck and into the store before Rafe could stop him! I (after he had run 3 laps around Walgreens) got him to stand in line with me. The guy behind me in line said, "Wow! I would love to have that much energy." (Yes, of course, the store was busy at the time!) I replied, "You and me, both! You ought to try keeping up with him!" Then he said, "Oh, I can't even imagine!" I really appreciate it when people actually talk to us instead of just staring at Walker like he is some sort of alien! Walker doesn't care, but it means a lot to me. I know it looks strange to see a 14 year old boy with a mustache running around Walgreens in his night-clothes and socks (at least he had that on!), but he is still my baby and I love him! And before you think I am some sort of saint, you should know that I was ready to kill him this morning when he woke up early and then woke his sister up! Ugggghhh! Ooops—time to get ready for church!

Feb 23, 2009 3:15pm

I got my blood work done this morning. No real change to my white blood cell count. Nurse said it was close to baseline but the doctor went ahead and ordered the Neupogen shot for me. I had one today and will get another in the morning. The only problem is that this can cause bone pain and/or flu like symptoms. Not looking forward to that. I have felt so great that I hate to jinx it.

I was studying my new Bible while I was at the doctor's office. I recently purchased one that is the New Living Translation. Not sure how I feel about it yet. It is a little different than the one I am used to which is the NIV. Anyway, in the front of this Bible, there is a section called, "How to Know Jesus Personally." #4 caught my eye. It says—God's plan brings peace. "I am leaving you with a gift—peace of mind and heart. And the peace I give is a gift the world cannot give. So don't be troubled or afraid" John 14:27. So, I looked this up. What I found very interesting was in John 14:30—"I don't have much more time to talk to you for the ruler of this world approaches. He has no power over me, but I will do what the Father requires of me, so that the world will know that I love the Father." Jesus is saying that he doesn't have to be arrested, condemned and crucified in that the law has *no* authority over him. *But*, God wants him to go through those things and he will do as the Father asks. So, for those who think it might be possible to get to the Father any other way, then *why* would God ask Jesus to go through all of that? Why not just preach that people should follow the law?

Feb 24, 2009 7:10pm

I got the 2nd Neupogen shot today. I felt fine so I went shopping immediately after instead of heading home to get a couple of Tylenol. Big mistake. I began to feel really achy like I was getting the flu. I took Tylenol as soon as I got home and began to feel better. Now I just feel really tired.

Gotta go tend to Hope. More later.

Feb 26, 2009 11:40am

I had a rough night after my 2nd Neupogen shot. I had a ton of bone pain from my rib cage, back, and down my legs. I fell asleep watching TV, and Rafe was sweet to let me go to bed while he tended to the kids. I think it was a late night for him. Luckily, sleep helped me get through those rough hours. I woke up on Wednesday feeling better but still a little achy. All of that bone pain was a good sign. My white blood cell count went from 1,000 to 1199. (These are approximate #s.)

Yesterday's chemo treatment went well. My friend Sara took me. We had a little bit of excitement as an older gentleman came in to get his Procrit shot at the same time as us. He was carrying his oxygen tank. His color did not look good. He sat down in the chair and was obviously not getting enough oxygen. The nurse took his pulse. It was at 40. They called 911 and had the ambulance take him to the hospital. Of course, he did not want to go. Sara and I were glad that they didn't listen to him. I know it was difficult for Sara to watch all of that. Her dad passed away last summer. He had emphysema.

After they got the gentleman taken care of, the nurse came to get my blood drawn, but my port was not working properly. I don't really understand it, but from what I gather, the port can get a small scab formed inside that will then act as a valve. She had to put in some medicine to dissolve that scab. Then it worked like a charm. They do flush the port before and after and sometimes between bags.

I'm feeling great today. Hope and I are headed to the book sale down at Trinity and Josey in a little while.

I keep thinking about the Tim McGraw song—Live like you are dying. If you listen to country music, you'll know the one I'm talking about. I heard it the other day when Walker and I were watching country videos. You know Walker and his country music! This song is about a man who gets a diagnosis of a life-threatening illness. The singer asks the man what he did next and he says, "I went sky diving, Rocky Mountain climbing" ... and went so many seconds on a bull. I've heard that song a lot of times and thought that must be a pretty honest message about what it is like to get that kind of a diagnosis. Now I know better. When I heard the cancer word, I thought, "Well this is it. This is how I'm going out." I always thought that if I ever found out I was dying, I would want to travel and see things I've never seen before. Trust me, all of that went out the window. All I wanted to do was spend as much time as I could with my precious Walker and Hope and Rafe and my parents and my sisters and family and friends. I thought about those I love who have still not turned their lives over to Christ. I wondered if this would do it for them or turn them farther away. I wondered if Hope would even remember me and if there was anything I could do to make sure that she would. And of course, I thought about what would happen to Walker. Who would take care of him? Rafe could not possibly do it on his own. I'm sorry if I've made any of you cry. That is not my intent. I just want to record an honest account of what I've gone through.

Of course, I honestly feel that God has heard all of the cries and prayers of my loved ones and has decided that yes, I have unfinished work on this earth yet to accomplish, and so, He's gonna let me stick around a while longer. That means a lot more evangelizing. Sorry for those of you who are sick of hearing it, but there is one way to make me stop. You know what you've gotta do! And if you don't, ask me!

I love all of you!

6

Feb 26, 2009 6:24pm

I almost forgot to post this important update!!! The doctor said the tumor is softening and shrinking in the breast!!! He could barely feel it in the lymph nodes—just one tiny spot. Praise God!!!

Feb 27, 2009 12:07pm

Just when I began to think it wouldn't happen, it has! I took a shower this morning and began to lose my hair. It's not coming out in huge chunks yet but enough to know it isn't my usual hair loss. And every time I scratch my head or run my fingers threw it, more comes out. So, I'm trying to leave it alone.

I can already see that it is going to be a huge mess. I will probably do as some others who have traveled this road before me have done—shave it! I will probably wait a couple of days before I do that.

I was hoping to get to spend this weekend with my sisters in Canton at the big flea market, but as we forgot to plan and since it is going to be cold, I guess we'll have to plan that for next month. I will probably be wearing that wig full time by then.

Hope and I went to church last night for our special needs support group meeting. I always have so much fun at those meetings. Yes, you read it correctly, we have fun. I also always come home feeling refreshed, renewed, and *loved!* I love you guys and girls!

I shared this prayer request with the group last night, but I want to post it here as well. We have signed up to go to Joni and Friends Family Retreat this summer. Joni and Friends is Christian organization for people with disabilities and their families. The Family Retreat is the highlight of our year! We get to go have fun and be loved on! We have our spot, but now comes the prayer part—please pray that my cancer treatment (which will by then be once every 3 weeks) will fall in just the right part of the month so that by the time we go to the retreat, I will feel well enough to have a great time and not be sick. Even though it is a relaxing time for us, it is still work to get us all there and also the nights can be difficult with Walker. So I really need to be feeling well to be able to handle it. We will be going the week of July 4th (not sure of the exact dates right now). About 10 or more families from our church will be going, plus even more volunteers!

Here is just a reminder regarding my treatment: First phase is Taxol, once a week for 12 weeks. Second phase is FEC, once every 3 weeks for 4 months. That should take us to the end of August or so. Then I will have surgery in September to have both breasts removed and also my ovaries removed as well. They will begin the reconstruction part during that surgery. I have a feeling I will really need the help (and prayers) in September, so please, don't wear yourselves out before then!

I love you all!

Feb 28, 2009 1:18pm

Hope has pink-eye. She started complaining last night while we were eating at Chili's. (Walker was *excellent* there, by the way—a little loud, but hey, it's Chili's. He didn't even have his music with him.) Her pediatrician's office was open this morning because it is flu season, so Rafe took her. The last place I need to be is in the waiting room of the pediatrician's office. The doctor confirmed what I suspected and prescribed an antibiotic and some eye drops. She feels just bad enough to be a pain in the you-know-where but not bad enough to go lay down! Uggghhhh! I am really praying that Walker does not come down with it as he is *sooo* difficult to get eye drops in his eyes! What a nightmare that would be! Pray for him and me!

Hair continues to fall out. It's not a hair shower yet but just a steady dropping.

7

*March 2009 came roaring in like a lion and took my
mane with it. My white blood cell counts dropped too
low requiring us to postpone chemo for a few days at
least twice. I got a few new wigs and learned to love
the ease of getting ready in the morning.*

*During this month, just like most of the others, we
saw God's miracles come in the form of friends rushing to our rescue.*

March 1, 2009 12:26pm

Not sure what key I hit but the entire thing I just
typed got deleted! Maybe that was God's way of
editing me.

Today is the day! Today is the day that I do the
unthinkable—I hand the clippers to Rafe and say,
"shave it!" I now have a waterfall of hair coming
off! All of those loose hairs are driving me crazy—
you know, that just-had-a-haircut feeling! Only, I
can't just take a shower to get rid of it. I'll let you
know if I cry during the shaving experience.

Hope is feeling much better today. Rafe and Walker
are at church this morning. The pediatrician said
Hope needs to stay home for one more day! Then
she can go to school tomorrow.

I have heard Stephen Curtis Chapman's song "Speechless" twice in the last 2 days. Walker and I both love S.C.C., and we really love that song. I have that CD around here somewhere and will attempt to find it today. I think it is appropriate since I sit at this computer trying to write things that, for one, reflect what I am experiencing with cancer but, more importantly, reflect what God has done for me. And despite all of the words I type, the truth is, nothing I write can do Him justice. The Truth is too good for words and in the end, I'm just left speechless! Stephen and his wife lost a child recently due to a terrible accident, and yet, he remains strong in his faith knowing that one day, he will see that child again.

One of the first songs that Walker loved of SCC's was "Fingerprints of God." I'm not sure if it was the melody he liked or if he identified with the message. I can certainly see Walker in that song and can see the fingerprints of God *all* over Walker!

"I can see the fingerprints of God when I look at you. I can see the fingerprints of God and I know it's true—You're a masterpiece that all creation quietly applauds and you're covered with the fingerprints of God!"

March 1, 2009 6:16pm

It is done! A 1 on the clippers was the shortest Rafe or I could stomach. It is pretty thin all over and now my head is really cold. I think I need some more head wraps. Clearly the two I bought will not be enough.

Do I like it? *No!* Am I crying? *No!* The good thing about having my kids is that they don't leave me a lot of time to feel sorry for myself. I have no choice but to get over it!

By the way, Rafe said I look like Sigourney Weaver in Aliens—ready to kick some alien butt! In this case, the alien is cancer.

March 4, 2009 3:48pm

My dear friend Cindy D. came to pick me up this morning to take me to my chemotherapy appointment. When we got there, they ran my blood as usual and found that my white blood cell count had dropped a significant amount since last week, soooo no chemo today. I got my Venu (iron) and a Neupogen shot and after 2 hours, we were on our way. The silver lining to this story is that Cindy and I actually got to go out to lunch instead of eating it in the chemo lounge. (I'm so blessed to have so many faithful and loyal friends!)

I go back for another Neupogen shot tomorrow morning and then it's back to the Chemo lounge on Friday morning where they will run my blood counts again and (Pray hard!) those counts will be up significantly so that I can still get my chemo this week. We don't want to give that cancer a chance to breathe at all! The Neupogen worked extremely well last week. I'm sure it can and will work this week as well.

The odd thing to me is that I felt better this past weekend than I have in all the previous ones. Good thing Dr. Saez and his staff are so diligent about checking those blood counts.

So, Loved Ones, here is the part of my post when I ask for your prayers. Pray for my white blood cell count and my neutrophils to go up and *stay* up! With chemo, you can usually expect them to go down, *But* we know that with God, we can expect the unexpected! With Him, it is possible for those counts to be normal and *stay* normal. Nothing is impossible when He is involved. And I know He is involved here. I know God loves me, because— from messages and meals to gifts and prays and from phone calls and shopping trips to sitting with me *all* day long during chemo—you all have shown me His love in a million ways . God bless you all!

March 6, 2009 4:05pm

I am still a little loopy from the Benadryl but since Hope is with my Mom & Dad and Walker is still at school, I will take this opportunity to sit down and write.

I did get my chemo today. The Neupogen worked again but it just barely worked. The first time I took the Neupogen, my white blood cell count was around 5 to start and then the Neupogen shot it to 18. Reference range is from 4 to 8. On Wednesday when I went in, it was at 2. (Rafe just came in. There goes the quiet.) Today after 2 Neupogen shots, it was at 5.49. That is really considered borderline but they went ahead and gave me chemo anyway. They gave me a smaller dose this time. Also my liver enzymes were up. The nurse said that was common but they want to keep an eye on it and that is another reason for the smaller dose. I am to go back in on Monday to have my counts checked again. If they are low, I will get 2 more days of Neupogen and then hopefully, chemo again on Wednesday. I see the doctor again on Wednesday. I am looking to see if there is anything I can do naturally to raise those counts. My doctor and the nurses say no, but I know lots of people use vitamins and diets to help when they are getting chemo. I know the glutathione and B12 seems to be helping with the neuropathy. Please pray on this issue.

Hope is home, so I will write more later!

Love to all,
Tracy

March 7, 2009 1:31pm

Happy Saturday! Hope and I just got back from the wig store with my sister, Jenny (aka Gege). She bought me two hair pieces on Monday and they came in today. I am calling them the Larry Feine (sp?) look. They just hang down from the head with straps across the scalp and need a scarf or hat or wrap over the top to hide your skull. The advantage to them is that they look like hair but are a lot cooler than a regular wig (and are a lot cheaper). I am wearing a long blond one today with a pink bandana. Rafe thinks I look like a hippie. I am calling this one the Ferf because I look a lot like my niece Jennifer in it. We call her The Ferf! My long dark wig (that looked a lot redder in the store when we bought it) makes me look a lot like my sister Laura, so I am calling it the Laurie. The other one is shorter and curly so I will call it the Gege. Now I just need a shorter blond to call the Joby after my sister, Joy, whom I call Joby. I think I have one picked out but just need to order it. Of course, I look the most like Joby normally so I guess my normal hair is the Joby.

I bought some Beta Glucon which is supposed to raise your white blood cell count and some Well-ness Formula which contains Vitamins A & C and Pau D'Arco to help do the same. I am praying that this will do the trick. I am feeling great today by the way.

"Which is easier: to say to the paralytic, 'Your sins are forgiven,' or to say, 'Get up, take your mat and walk'? But that you may know that the Son of Man has authority on earth to forgive sins..." he said to the paralytic, "I tell you, get up, take your mat and go home." Mark 2:9-11 (NIV)

March 8, 2009 12:02pm

Water heater went out this morning. This is the 2nd time with this water heater which we replaced just about 5 years ago. Last time it was the valve that we had to order and wait a week to get in the mail and get my father-in-law here to install. (We paid a plumber last time to come and tell us there was nothing he could do.) This time it could be the same thing or it could be just the thermal coupling. Rafe stripped the nut this morning when trying to get it off. Rafe *hates* working on plumbing which is why he did not join the plumbing business. So, as you can imagine, he is in a very bad mood.

This is the kind of thing that gets to me! It is really just an inconvenience and yet, being without hot water and having a grumpy husband is *not* fun!!! Adding this on to our other troubles just makes life really difficult!

March 8, 2009 6:28pm

Still no hot water. Rafe would rather wait until his dad can bring us a new one next weekend. So, no hot water for an entire week. I'm thrilled, can you tell?

Allergies really bothering me. I'm tired. My house is a wreck. I think I'm going to bed.

March 9, 2009 9:37am

I'm having a hard time right now, emotionally. Cumulative effect of everything, I guess. Rafe asked me yesterday afternoon what was wrong. I said, "Do you want the entire list or just the top 3!" Funny how you can struggle and see the light when battling autism. Then you can see the light when battling cancer. You can even trust that your loved ones are in God's hands, but then a stupid little thing like being without hot water can knock you on your rear end and into total darkness. Ridiculous, I know.

It is *not* so much the fact that the hot water heater is out. It is more the fact that it is out *again*. And the fact that Rafe and I can't afford to have a plumber just come and install a new water heater. I really thought that by 42 my life would be a little different. I'm just doing the same things and also dealing with autism and breast cancer. *Fun!* The silver lining here of course is that when I take my bath in

1 inch of heated up water, I don't have to wash my hair!!!

Sorry for the negative tone this morning, but it is how I am feeling. When Hope and I were in the car this morning on the way to school, I heard a song on the radio that made a thought pop into my head and I said, "Hey Hope! Do you know that when we get to heaven, Walker will be able to talk to us? He will no longer have a bobo (as we call it) on his brain." She said, "*Yes*! I know! He can tell us what he wants and what he's thinking! That will be great!" She at 4 gets it while I at 42 still have to be reminded! Oh, the song says (sorry but I don't know the title) "there will be no more tears, no more fears...." (And plenty of hot water!)

Today's verse:

"I am the true vine, and my Father is the gardener. He cuts off every branch in me that bears no fruit, while every branch that does bear fruit he prunes so that it will be even more fruitful." John15:1-2 (NIV)

March 9, 2009 8:18pm

We have hot water!!! Thank you to all of the little angels at our church and elsewhere (you know who you are!) for making it possible for us all to take hot baths tonight—without heating the water on the stove first! We love you! (And I would say that even if we didn't have hot water tonight. But, I'm really, really glad that we do!)

I had another Neupogen shot today. Dr. Saez said one shot should be enough, but we will see on Wednesday when I have blood work done again.

March 11, 2009 9:04pm

I was able to get my chemo today but again at a much smaller dose. My liver enzymes were down by half which is good, and my white blood cell count was within the normal range. Dr. Saez said that my blood counts have been crazy because my liver has not been doing its job. Now that it is healing, my blood counts have stabilized. I will go in again on Monday to have my blood counts checked again. *If* my liver enzymes have continued to decrease, then he will increase my Taxol to halfway between the dose I am getting now and the full dose. Then we will slowly increase it to get to the full dose. He said it is common for the Taxol to wreak havoc on the liver. It is a toxin, after all!

The really, really good news is that he could barely find the tumor today!!! Thank you, Jesus! I know, Jesus, that you know which path is best for me. Regardless of the outcome I love you and I praise you! But I do thank you for this good news!

I am feeling tired tonight but that is all. Hope is already asleep (Walker is not, of course) so I think I am going to go to bed.

Oh, something cool Walker said today. Hope yelled out to me, "Where's Daddy?" And without missing a beat, Walker yelled out, "He's at work!" We all praised him, because Rafe was in fact at work! He is on fire tonight (figuratively speaking, that is)!!! I wish I could bottle whatever is working in him tonight!

Rafe and I have decided to now start selling advertising space in my journal! Hey, we have doctors to pay! :-) And on that silly note, I'm out!

March 14, 2009 10:24pm

I haven't updated in a couple of days, so while the house is relatively quiet, I thought I would write down a few thoughts.

Rafe's mom and dad are here this weekend. Rafe and his dad (mostly his dad) put down laminate flooring in Hope's bedroom. We have the same stuff in our room and liked it so much we decided to put it in hers as well. It looks great!

While the men are working on home projects, I have enjoyed visiting with my mother-in-law. Rafe and I are so blessed to have parents on both sides who are so supportive of us and very giving. I can't imagine what we would have done over our 18 years of marriage without the love and support coming from both sides.

I can't remember if I posted before, but I have been fighting a cold now for over a week. I tried to convince myself that it was just allergies, but I finally had to admit the truth. My oncologist gave me a script for a Z pack (antibiotics) just in case the cold/cough had any thoughts about turning into an infection. With my white blood cells low, that can happen pretty quickly. I feel fine now though, other than the stupid cough that is relentless. On top of that, Walker and Hope now both have it. They both woke up several times last night from that cough.

It is so hard for me to imagine being able to get well when I get so very little sleep. It's not the fact that we don't get to bed until late but more of the interruptions throughout the night that really stink! We see reports on the news constantly about how bad the lack of sleep is for you. Rafe and I always yell at the TV, *"Yes, we know!"* And that was before we knew I had cancer! And if the kids aren't waking us up, it's our cat!

So much for the quiet. I've got to get Hope to bed!!!

March 15, 2009 2:58pm

The sun has made an appearance today for the first time in 5 days. It is a shame my mother-in-law and father-in-law had to head home today. I pray that they don't have any problems on their trip home. I also pray that we get some beautiful weather for spring break!

Ephesians 2:4-5: "But because of his great love for us, God, who is rich in mercy, made us alive with Christ even when we were dead in transgressions—it is by grace you have been saved."

Steve, one of the associate pastors filled in for Pete today at church. He discussed Ephesians 2:4-5. He asked the question—what does grace mean to you? Here is my answer:

God's grace for me means that when I heard the words breast cancer and thought the end of this life was near, while I worried about my kids being without their mom, I did not worry about me. I didn't spend a single second thinking about anything I may have done right or wrong in this life.

Instead, I thought about what it will be like when I will go home to my Father and rest in His arms. What a glorious day that will be!!!

So, you should know that when I fight for my life, I do so with some reservation. What waits for me in heaven I know is far better than my life here. But, rest assured, I will fight. Partly because my kids need me, but mostly because I feel that it is what my God in Heaven wants me to do at this time. There will be time for rest later—much later!

March 16, 2009 2:43pm

Went for blood work appt. My wbc count was again low and so was given another Neupogen shot. I go in for another tomorrow and then back for chemo on Wednesday. They won't get my liver test back until tomorrow and so will find out tomorrow how that is going.

I also have a cold sore. Lovely! Otherwise feeling fine and cough is getting better. Today is the last day for my antibiotics. Walker still not feeling too well.

My hair (the little stubble that is left of it) continues to fall out at a pretty steady rate. Those tiny hairs can drive a person crazy! I can't stop scratching my head!!!

March 17, 2009 11:12pm

I asked the nurse today when I went in for my 2nd Neupogen shot if she had given me the extra strength version yesterday! Ohhhhhh! I have felt so achy and tired since that first shot. The first one usually doesn't affect me this severely. Of course, if I'm hurting, it is working so I'm not complaining. Okay, maybe I am.

While I was at the doctor's office, the nurse took one look at my fever blister and said, "Oh, Dr. Saez needs to give you something for that." So I came home with a script for Acyclovir. Apparently when you are on chemo, everything is a big deal!

I took a good long nap this afternoon, courtesy of my very sweet and kind husband! He worked with Walker and the Occupational therapist while Hope and I took a nap. Hope's nap was by force! (She was in trouble and got sent to her room and accidentally fell asleep while she was in there. I thought autism was tough! This normal kid business is so difficult!)

We were up half the night last night with both kids. When Walker was diagnosed with autism, I re-member being so incredibly mad at God. (Funny but I never doubted God's existence at that time. I've had my moments of doubt at other times but not then.) With my cancer diagnosis, I have not yet felt any anger towards God. I'm not saying I won't at some point, but I haven't yet. I thought one of two scenarios were in motion. Either God was calling me home and was using cancer to do it or He wasn't in which case He would heal me. Either way, He knows best. *But* (and here is the big but...) last night, and many other nights when Walker has been up and he's making noise and keeping one or both or all of us up, it is so difficult not to be mad at God. I still don't know what He is thinking at those times. I know, I know, what doesn't kill you makes you stronger and God never gives you more than you can handle. That, by the way, is a big crock! He frequently gives you more than you can handle so that you will learn to let HIM handle it! Okay, so perhaps I just answered my own question. Maybe those nights when Walker won't sleep and Rafe and I feel like we just can't make it another second, maybe God is saying "Rest in Me! Let Me give you a peace beyond all understanding." I still say that 2:00 am is not really a good time to try to teach me anything!

March 19, 2009 11:44 PM, CDT

New photos uploaded including one that I would *only* show to my very closest of friends! Posting that photo of me with my buzzed head is what I call brave!

Thursday, March 19, 2009 11:22 AM, CDT

I got my chemo yesterday. Reference range for white blood cell count is between 4 and 11, mine was 27!!! The nurse said my body thought it was fighting off a major infection which is why I felt so bad. My liver function is normal or almost normal again, so they were able to increase my Taxol dose by a little bit. Hurray!

Other than the kids driving us crazy, life is good once again at the McCain household!

March 21, 2009 6:46 PM, CDT

I felt sick last night—from allergies, perhaps—and so took medicine that knocked me out!!! Poor Rafe was left to deal with these 2 kids on his own. I feel better today, but I am still a little worn out. Is any-one else suffering from allergies? Ugghhh!

I have completed 7 weeks of Chemo. I have 5 more to go of the 12 week course. My last of the Taxol will be around April 22nd (that is if all goes accord-ing to plan). Then I will begin on the FEC which is another chemo drug. I will get the FEC once every 3 weeks for 4 months. I'm not sure when in April or May I will get the first of it. That takes us to August. So, surgery should be some time at the end of Au-gust or the first of September. At least with getting chemo in the spring/summer months, I don't have to worry about my head getting cold. I just have to worry about sunburn!!!

As I mark off weeks on my calendar, I am reminded of when I marked weeks of my pregnancies on the calendar. Those were much happier weeks. (And I was a lot fatter and had a lot more hair!)

March 23, 2009 11:44 AM, CDT

I'm feeling well today. I'm trying to play catch up with all of those things I didn't get done during Spring break. So far, I seem to be just spinning my wheels.

Every day I hear from someone who tells me that they are reading this journal. I am absolutely amazed at how many people read this journal on a regular basis. I have to say that it makes me kind of nervous. I mean, why would anyone put any stock at all in anything I have to say? But I received a message from the Holy Spirit yesterday that made me laugh! I started thinking about this very topic while driving. Yes, I know these things always occur to me while driving which should prompt you to get out of my way if you see me coming from the other direction. I thought, I really hope I don't disappointment people out there who expect to read something worthwhile. I don't know what I'm talking about!!! Honestly!

Then it hit me — if God decides to use this journal to talk to even one person, wouldn't that be marvelous!!! And if that is the case, it doesn't really matter what I type. I could just type gibberish and God will make sure that person gets the message loud and clear. Isn't He amazing??? I have to admit, that idea sure took a lot of pressure off of me. I will still do my best to be my clever little self, but I will rest in the knowledge that I can't possibly screw up anything the Big Guy has to say!

March 26, 2009 9:18 PM, CDT

Eight Taxols down, 4 more to go. Tumor is shrinking. Liver is looking good. White blood cell count and neutrophils back up after the Neupogen. Benadryl still makes me *very* sleepy which is why we did not go to Special Needs group tonight at church. On the flip side, the Benadryl really helped my allergies today. My cough is better today than it has been in a week. That tells me it is definitely allergies.

I have such spring fever! I just want to get in the car and go someplace!!! (Just don't want to have to deal with kids on the trip. I love them, but....)

Oh, and I ordered another wig online. This one is short and blond. Yikes! Makes me a little nervous to order it online, but it was very inexpensive and was one I've seen for a lot more money in the salons. If I like it, you'll be seeing it. If not, well....

I haven't posted anything in a while. Sunday was a rough day for me emotionally. My bad mood had very little to do with cancer but instead had to do with Walker's autism. Weekends are tough, as my fellow autism moms out there know. Trying to find enough to keep these kids busy is a real chore. Add cold weather, wind, cancer ... forget about it! Walker tends to have severe mood swings so even if you keep him busy, he can be bouncing off the walls one minute and then crying the next.

I have gotten 2 more Neupogen shots this week, so I am feeling tired, achy, and cranky. I was able to go to a new Bible study that has just started up with some friends of mine from church. We are studying Jennifer Rothschild's *Me, Myself, & Lies*. It is all about the lies that the enemy whispers in your ear and then you let come out your lips. Women tend to do this a lot. For example, we often tell ourselves, "I'm not good enough, or smart enough, or pretty enough."

At church, we're still studying Ephesians 2 and this week covered Ephesians 2:10. "For we are God's masterpiece. He has created us anew in Christ Jesus, so that we can do good things he planned for us long ago." (NLV) Reading this and then studying the *Me, Myself, & Lies* book, I can't help but think about the heroes of the Bible who did not believe that they were good enough (or smart enough, or strong enough) to carry out God's work. Moses, Jonah, Noah were convinced that they couldn't do it! It seems funny to imagine these great men doubting themselves. Of course, few of us will ever complete tasks as grand as these three, but in the scheme of God's kingdom, all tasks are important. Please, do not think for one minute that I am comparing myself to Moses, or Noah, or even Jonah. Far from it!!! But, I do see myself as one of God's masterpieces! I know He has been working on me for a long time. I know He has a task for all of us, but I think He has blessed me to let me see His hand pushing me / using me towards some goal. I may not know what that goal is until I get to heaven, but I know it is close at hand.

He has already demonstrated a great deal of love through all of you. Our Pastor, talked about the lady he met in Wisconsin who told him a story about a lady from our church whom she met while visiting. She was in the lobby and asked a lady if she could help her find a phone to call a cab. The lady went one better and gave her a ride to the airport. The Pastor talked about how that task had been prepared for her long before she was even born. It was a very simple task but it was important to God's Kingdom. Okay, so, now think of all of the meals, cards, phone calls, presents, rides, groceries, and I'm sure I can't remember all of the things we have received from all of you since my diagnosis. All of those were tasks that God prepared for each of you way before any of us were even on this earth. And they were all designed to show Christ's love! Wow! As the song says, I'm still amazed!!!

8

In April 2009 I continued with my chemotherapy treatments despite a few scares regarding my liver enzyme levels. We celebrated Easter, and we discussed summer plans. And as usual, Mama's work does not stop for chemo.

April 1, 2009 8:57 PM, CDT

Got chemo today!! WBC and neutrophils were way high—praise God, Neupogen works!!! Had fun at chemo today as usual visiting with my peeps! Another friend came up to meet me and Sara, and brought lunch. The nurses always laugh at me. I tell them, "You know Wednesdays are my social days!" They say, "Yes, we know you enjoy your Wednesdays!" :-) And the more people keep hearing about how much fun we have, the more people want in on the fun! :-) What a gift the Lord has given me! Friends who fight over me!!! Thank you Jesus! There is *no* doubt in my mind that Jesus loves me *so big!*

Okay, now here is a really cool God story that I get to share with all of you! Get ready to feel goose bumps! (BTW, I think goose bumps happen when you get a very close up look at God.) So, I'm sitting here tonight doing our taxes when the phone rings.

73

When I answer it, the lady on the other end explains that her husband owns a business that installs windows and home siding and would we like a quote? I explain to her that right now I have NO money as I have a child with autism and I have cancer. She says, "Really? I used to teach special education years ago and children with autism." Then she asks, "What is your son's name? I will pray for him." So I tell her and she says, "I will pray. You should expect great things for him." I say thanks and we hang up. Then I got strong tug from the Holy Spirit and so I stopped and prayed for her business. "Lord, please give this husband and wife a lot of work. Grow their business and let them put a lot of people to work!" Then I get another push by the Holy Spirit and so, I dial *69 to get her phone number because I forgot to ask the first time. I call her back, she answers right away, and I told her that I had just prayed for her business and would like the name and # of her business because one day I will need to get new windows for my house. So the business is Beck Exteriors. Their names are Trey and Cindy. She told me that she would put a star by my name and tell her husband to give me a rock bottom price! What nice people!!!

Feeling loved! Feeling very loved!!!

April 4, 2009 11:53 AM, CDT

Battling normal mom stuff this morning. Found out yesterday that Hope has strep throat again. I'm worried that Walker will come down with it too since it is so contagious and he and Hope usually share such things. Hope's doctor did give us a little extra antibiotic to give Walker just in case he comes down sick this weekend before I can get him to the doctor.

I also worry that I will come down with it. I managed to avoid it the last 2 times the kids had it, but I didn't have low white blood cell count then. Lots of hand washing.

Just 3 more Taxols left. Then I start the 2nd phase of chemo.

April 5, 2009 3:09 PM, CDT

Happy Palm Sunday!

Our pastor, Pete, asked us to write down what the scripture spoke to us today. We read from Mark 10 & 11. I have thought and thought, but came up with nothing from the scripture. Maybe I'm trying too hard instead of letting the Lord speak to me. One thing that did cross my mind today did not come from the Word but instead from a little funny film they showed today at church. The film was about Lifegroups or Mini churches or small groups (all the same thing). They really want everyone to be connected in some way. In a church our size, if you don't belong to a smaller group, you kind of get lost. It would be very easy to go to church on Sunday and never know a single other person at Bent Tree. The film showed a guy who belonged to a mini church of 1. It was really cute as it showed him doing all the things a small group does, but he did all of those things by himself. Rafe and I would be a group of 2 if God hadn't intervened for us. We are just not joiners. I know, that may come as a shock to some of you. But really, if we didn't have Walker, we might not have ever gotten saved much less gotten involved. But, God made it clear to us that we need others. He didn't give us a choice. Our small group is our special needs group. These are the people with whom we do life. We didn't choose to be members. God chose us! I am so incredibly glad that God did! I can't imagine where or what we would be without Bent Tree, our fellow special needs friends, and our Lifeguards who make it possible to go to service and to meetings! Love you all!

A friend sent me a book called Praying through Cancer. It is sooo excellent. It is a Daily Devotional written by women who have battled cancer. I really like that it is a devotional and not just another secular book written about cancer. The very first entry was written by Rick Warren's wife. She talks about how even though the cancer was a surprise for her, it was not a surprise for God. God was preparing for that diagnosis long in advance. He was giving her everything she would need to fight it long before she knew anything about it. When I think about being here in Carrollton now, I know this is how it is for me. Rafe and I really did not want to move here. We were happy in Corpus Christi, but we knew that we had to do whatever we could for Walker. Once again, we did for Walker but God did for us! We went to our church because we thought it was the best church for Walker. Before I was even born, God was preparing for this battle. He aligned everything just perfectly for us for His purpose. And again, regardless of the outcome, I know that His purpose will be fulfilled and that He has given us everything we need. What an awesome God!

I got Chemo yesterday and saw the doctor. He asked questions about how I'm feeling. I have no noticeable neuropathy; a few issues with acid reflux; and no other major issues on my end. My liver enzymes were up again slightly so he is going to decrease the Taxol dose down a little again. He had increased it slightly when the enzyme levels had gone down but now will go back to the decreased dose size. He said that just means my body does not need as much. My reflexes are good. The super good news is that he couldn't really find my tumor. He found one spot that *could* be it but it was so faint that he wasn't sure.

I only have 2 more Taxols left so he said for these next 2, I am to come in on Mondays for blood draw and Neupogen shot if needed. I will not need to get one on Tuesdays as 1 seems to do the trick. (Yippee!) Then back on Wednesdays for chemo and no need to check blood then, which is really surprising and good news.

My last Taxol dose will be on April 22nd. Then I get a whole week off! I begin the FEC (which is actually 3 chemo drugs) on May 6th. With this chemo, I will also get the Aloxi for nausea. It's the one that lasts for 5 days. I will also get Emends which is another drug for nausea and according to my friend, Ronda, is an absolute Godsend! (Ronda, by the way, is getting her last chemo treatment this week! My prayers are with ya, sista'!) I will also get a shot called Neulasta to keep my blood counts from dropping drastically. I have heard this is a very affective drug but also causes some pretty gnarly bone pain. And I believe it costs $7500 per shot! Thank God for insurance and for a total out of pocket which we have now met! I will get the FEC every 3 weeks for 4 months, but I believe I will still have to go get the Herceptin weekly. I will be on the weekly Herceptin for an entire year.

I told my oncologist about our plans to attend the Joni and Friends Family Retreat (for people with special needs and their families) this summer, so he and I looked at the calendar and counted it out. If all goes as planned, there should be no problems with us going to camp. In fact, we will be at camp the weekend before my very last treatment. What a reason to celebrate!!

I also discussed the hot flashes I've been having with the oncologist. Chemo stops you from ovulating which then causes hot flashes. Oh, the joy never ends. They're not horrible yet but plenty annoying. He said there are several medications we can try that do not involve hormones. I told him that I will get back to him when I feel they are bad enough to try something.

At the end of this month, I will go for another echo-cardiogram to check my heart. Please pray for that to go well. I will also go back to see my surgeon and get in to see a plastic surgeon to discuss reconstruction surgery. The reconstruction surgery is usually 6 months after the initial surgery.

So, all good news at this point. The greatest news is

that while the Taxol has been really easy on me, it has done quite the number on my cancer! Of course, you and I know that it doesn't matter how great a medication is if the Lord is not with that medication. Well, He has been with this medication! He has his hand in there defeating the enemy, as usual! My hero, as always!!!

Not sure I will get a chance to update again before Easter, so if not, let me wish you all a very Happy Easter. Most of all, I want to once again thank my Lord and Savior for rescuing me—not from cancer but from a life of sin and darkness. The *light* is oh so much better!!!

I just want you to all know that I am now crying happy tears. I found some new features on this website, one of which allows me to see a list of those who have signed in to my guestbook and another list of those who have registered to receive update notices. I knew a lot of people were reading, but I had no idea how many! *Wow*! Well over 50 people check this site regularly! I am touched beyond words for the love and concern shown to me, to Rafe, and our family! Believe me, it means so much!!! God is in this place! (Wiping tears!!!)

Love to you all!
Tracy

9

April 17, 2009 1:34 PM, CDT

Sorry for the long absence. I've just been busy and haven't had much to report.

Walker was sick last weekend and was given a script for an antibiotic by his doc. He had a cough and some kind of secondary infection. I haven't ruled out a foreign object up his nose just yet as this has been an issue before. Haven't seen anything yet, so I am hoping it is gone (if that was in fact the problem).

I'm feeling great. I am down to only 1 more weekly treatment and then it's on to phase 2. I was thinking about how great I've done on the Taxol and I truly have no other explanation other than the fact that God is answering all of those prayers out there! I am so thankful! I am praying that Phase 2 goes as smoothly.

I am going tomorrow morning to a support group for people who share the breast cancer gene. My surgeon is presenting as is a plastic surgeon with whom she works. It should be interesting. I'll share any info I get.

81

April 23, 2009 10:37 PM, CDT

Twelve weeks of Taxol completed! Phew!!! Only 4 months left to go!

I get next week off and then on May 6th I start on FEC every 3 weeks. I will continue to get the Herceptin weekly until I am finished with chemo. Once I am done with chemo, they can increase the Herceptin dose and then administer it every 3 weeks until the year mark which was I believe January 30th. The Herceptin has to be taken an entire year.

As reported, last Saturday I went to the support group for people who share the breast cancer gene or family history. My surgeon spoke as did a plastic surgeon. It was interesting, informative, and overwhelming all at the same time. I think I left with more questions than answers in terms of how long my surgery will take and exactly how many surgeries I will need. The informative part was that they showed pictures of reconstructed breasts. I was happy to see that they all looked like real breasts and the scarring was minimal. The incisions are done underneath the breast so that the scar is then hidden under the breast. It was a relief to me because I had no idea what I was going to look like when this was all over. I am a woman and would like to continue to look like one. Even if they aren't real. My friend Laurie told me about a t-shirt and I actually saw it this week in a wig store that reads, "Yes, these are fake. The real ones were trying to kill me." I love it but I wouldn't have the guts to actually wear it. I'm pushing it with my "Got chemo?" shirt.

I was a little shaken by all of the sisters, aunts, moms and daughters who attended the meeting and all shared the cancer gene. So many of them had family members who had died from breast or ovarian cancer. I immediately left there and called all of my sisters urging them to go have the test done immediately. I know it might feel like it is scarier to know the truth, but trust me, having cancer is worse.

So, what has happened this week? Well, as usual, I went in on Monday for my blood draw and my Neupogen shot. No surprise that yes, my white blood cell counts were down and I needed the Neupogen. I only needed the Monday shot. I could still feel the effects of that shot in my bones on Wednesday when I went for chemo. So no surprise then that my counts were up high enough for chemo. Chemo on Wednesday went smoothly. Cindy and I tried to work on our Bible study but were too tempted to talk. Okay, Cindy will tell you that it was I who kept talking. And she'd be correct. Let's just say that Hope gets her verbal skills from her mother.

Hope has learned the word "chemo." I never meant to teach her the word. She just picked it up from hearing us. She told me the other day, "Just go get your chemo!" Not very nice, but there you have it! She has her moments and I try to remember that she is exactly who God wants her to be while at the same time remembering that it is my job to teach her to be a caring person. We're working on it. Just like me, she is a work in progress! Although, it is sometimes obvious to me that where Walker is concerned, she is already very advanced. Just the other day she said, "Momma, I know Walker has autism, but I don't care. He is my brother and I love him!" So precious!!! I wish I had it on tape for me to play back to her in the future when she gets frustrated and mad at him. But at least I have written them here now and will show this to her at those moments. I know she'll have them. I have them too.

April 24, 2009 3:17 PM, CDT

I had my 2nd echo-cardiogram this afternoon. I have no news yet as to how my heart looks.

I have added a couple of photos in the last couple of weeks, so check those out.

April 26, 2009 4:10 PM, CDT

Hi Loved Ones,

I'm doing some pretty heavy thinking for myself this weekend. Must be the weather. I am 42 years old. In the last 6 months before my diagnosis, I was just coming to grips with the fact that I am no longer in the "having babies" stage of my life. Yes, I have enough to take care of, thank you Lord! But for some reason, for women, this is a typical stage. I have the advantage of being the baby of 4 girls in my family, so I have seen my sisters all go through this stage. I am suddenly in the I AM NO LONGER YOUNG AND IN FACT, I COULD DIE phase. That is a *huge* step to take all at once. I know, I know, I'm getting better. I'm going to live. *But* with cancer, you just never know. *And* of course there is also the possibility that I could get hit by a bus tomorrow. I guess what I am trying to say is that there are just no guarantees where living on this earth are concerned, and I have come to that realization rather quickly. This fact should remind us that while there are no guarantees for life on this earth, there IS a guarantee where Christ Jesus is concerned!!! He has given me a *free* guarantee of life everlasting! And not just any life, a life full of joy with Him in Heaven! Praise God!!!

There is a song on Christian radio—sorry but the title escapes me at the moment, chemo brain, I guess—but one line says that we are all just one phone call away from being down on our knees. This always reminds me of the day my doctor called to give me the results of the biopsy. Yes, it is cancer—ductal carcinoma also in at least one lymph node. And down I go. Wouldn't it be wonderful if we could all get there without having to get that phone call first? And if and when you get that phone call, you are already on your knees. I want to get there soon.

Here I am on my knees with palms up!
Tracy

10

In May 2009, my second round of chemotherapy began. It was quite the change from Taxol given weekly to FEC (also known as "The Red Devil") given once every 3 weeks. While the Taxol was rather easy on my system, FEC was not. I discovered that I had not had a true chemo experience until this time. Praise God I had a wonderful doctor and a great support system. My hair, surprisingly, began to grow in again, only to begin falling out again later.

May 3, 2009 3:05 PM, CDT

I had an entire week off from all things cancer (chemo, Herceptin, blood work, etc.) and so also took an entire week off from this journal.

I worked a little. I ran some errands that needed runnin'. I played with Hope. Watched all the hysterics about the pig flu on the news. And otherwise just enjoyed my week. Mostly, I enjoyed *not* going to the doctor's office to get poked and prodded and chemoed. That ends this week.

I enjoyed church quite a bit this morning. We are still on Ephesians. (I know, how long can they talk about Ephesians?) Believe it or not, that small book of the Bible has a *big* message. I won't go into the whole sermon. If you'd like to look it up, today we covered Ephesians 2:14-20. Specifically, we as the body of Christ are more than just his church. We are called to be the Kingdom of God, the family of God, and the temple of God. Very interesting. There was one thing that Pete mentioned today that really struck me. He said that he met a member of our church whose family never went to church but one Sunday morning he woke up and said, "We need to go to church." They ended up at Bent Tree. One year later, the guy tells Pete, "Church is *not* at all what I expected." Pete asked, "What did you expect?" He stated that he expected to meet a lot of people there all dressed up and "playing church." Pete asked, "What did you find?" He stated, "Jesus!" To that, I say, Praise God!!! Thank you, Lord!!! That is exactly what I found at Bent Tree as well. Jesus is there! He changed me forever and I am so thankful for that. If you knew me before, you know this is true. He changed me but more importantly, He changed my heart.

Pete also mentioned that when you point people to Jesus enough, the devil gets really upset and starts to attack. (Funny, I think I said that last week. Maybe Pete reads my journal. :-) At any rate, Rafe and I must be doing something right, because we have been under attack from the enemy for quite some time now!!! And I know just what Pete meant when he said that you are then tempted to not point to Jesus so much so that the enemy will then decrease his attacks. But you just can't do that. I agree. I refuse to do that. Having said that—I rebuke the devil! I asked the Lord to fill every inch of my home with His spirit so that no evil can get in. I ask him to place angels around me and my family to protect us from the evil one. And I pray that He will keep His mighty and merciful hand on us morning, noon, and night! I pray this for my family here in my home, for my family elsewhere, and for my church family and friends. I pray this for anyone reading this journal.

One more thing, if any of you have been hanging on to the fence, and by that I mean, you have been putting off making the decision to not only accept Christ as your Savior but also to hand your life over to Him completely, I urge you to not put it off another second. You never know if you'll get another chance. Stephen Curtis Chapman has a song titled, The Invitation. Well, this is your invitation!!! Take it and use it!!! Open God's gift of Grace now!!! He's begging for you to!

May 4, 2009 6:47 PM, CDT

Hope's school is out this week due to the swine flu. So far there are no cases in Walker's school district, so he is still in school. Thank you Lord for that! I'd rather have the swine flu than stay home with Hope and Walker all week long! Okay, partially kidding.

Went to have my blood tested today. My white blood cell count is normal. My neutrophils were borderline but the Dr. said that should be up to normal by Wednesday, and so I am good to get chemo on Wednesday. I did not have to get a Neupogen shot today. Yeah!

Walker had a good weekend, but I am just exhausted. I guess 12 weeks of chemo finally caught up with me. I've just been really tired and grumpy. Hope fell asleep right before dinner and so most likely won't sleep tonight. Uggghhh!

Glad the rain has stopped for a while. I am ready to get on with my chemo. This may sound stupid, but I am cleaning my bathroom really well just in case I get sick on Wednesday night or Thursday morning. Everyone I've talked to has said to expect some pretty bad nausea from this round. I can't stand to be sick in a dirty bathroom! So, I'm preparing for the worst but praying for the best!

May 7, 2009 1:28 PM, CDT

Rafe went with me to chemo yesterday. Chemo itself was uneventful except that it took a long time mainly because the chemo lounge was very busy. We got there about 10:00 and got done at 2:30.

Unfortunately, as uneventful as the chemo experience was, last night was *not!* About 5:00 pm, I suddenly began to get nauseated. I felt like I had been hit by a truck. So, I sent Rafe to get my prescription for Zofran. We had dropped it off earlier in the day, thank goodness. The Zofran helped some. I was able to eat a little bit of spinach salad without it coming back up. I feel better this morning but feel like I have a hang-over. There is a reason I gave up drinking!!! I am afraid that the FEC will not be as easy on me as the Taxol was!

Here are my current meds:

Pre-meds —

Tylenol, Dekadron (steroid), Aloxi (5 day anti-nausea med), Benadryl, and Emends (for nausea)

Then the FEC, actually 3 different meds in three different IV bags fluorouracil, Epirubicin, Cyclophosphamide. The nurses call the Epirubicin the Red Devil because it is bright red. Within 1 hour of getting it, my urine was the same color! (Sorry, TMI, I know.)

Herceptin

I get the Emends with chemo and then I take it in pill version on day 2 and another on day 3. I also have the Zofran which is an 8 hour med and doesn't cause drowsiness. I can take the Phenergan, but it does cause you to get very sleepy.

I also had to go in today to get my Neulasta shot. It keeps my blood counts from dropping drastically but is supposed to cause bone pain. I have taken some Tylenol and feel okay not but will probably be hurting from that tonight.

When I saw the nurse today, she told me to come back in tomorrow if I am still nauseous and they will give me some more Aloxi. Hopefully I won't need it.

Please pray that tonight goes by without too much pain for me but lots of pain for cancer.

May 8, 2009 2:14 PM, CDT

I'm feeling a little better today, but I still have waves of nausea now and then. They are brief, thank goodness. The strangest problem I have today is muscle soreness. I can't figure that one out.

Both arms, shoulders, hips, and thighs are sore. I think I will call the doctor just to make sure that is normal.

Happy Mother's Day to all the moms out there! An especially big Happy Mother's Day to all the moms with children with special needs out there! I know how hard you work!

Love to all!
Tracy

May 8, 2009 6:20 PM, CDT

Hit a brick wall again this afternoon. The muscle aches I was feeling got progressively worse. I called the doctor and he blamed it on the Neulasta. I was expecting bone pain, so I was a little thrown off by the muscle aches. Strange since it started in my chest, then progressed to my shoulders and down my arms. It's now everywhere including my hips, bottom, and down my legs. I'm also exhausted. I got a short nap this afternoon, but Rafe kept coming in to "check" on me. :-)

Stomach is still queasy, and I'm suffering from indigestion as well. So, this is what chemo is really like. I must say ... I don't like it!!!

I just want to say a very Happy Mother's Day to two women who have set perfect examples to me of how a mom should be—my mom and my mother-in-law!!! I love you both!

May 10, 2009 9:04 PM, CDT

Feeling better today. Most of my achiness is gone. I do still get light headed which then makes me feel like I'm going to throw up, but it goes away quickly when I sit down. Even felt well enough to go out to my mom and dad's today to celebrate Mother's Day.

I was very sick yesterday!

May 18, 2009 12:18 AM, CDT

I feel back to my old self now. Well, my old self minus the hair. It has taken a while. I remained dizzy for a couple of days, especially after I ate. Not sure why. I continued to suffer for a couple more days with horrible acid reflux after I ate or drank *anything*. Even a glass of water would set it off. As a consequence of that, my throat was sore, even though I was taking Pepcid AC twice a day! That is gone now, thankfully, and I haven't needed the Pepcid in about 3 days. Yeah!!!

So now I get to enjoy this week free from chemo. I will need to go back to get my Herceptin again this Wednesday, but I have no side effects from that as far as I can tell. I head back for my next chemo on May 27th. I am praying that the side effects from this round are much less severe. However, I am also more aware of what will probably happen and so, will be ready. As ready as I can be that is.

I'll check back in later!

May 21, 2009 10:51 AM, CDT

On Sunday night, shortly after getting Walker settled down and then shutting off the computer, I headed to bed around 12:45. At approximately 1:15 am, I straight up and ran to the bathroom and

began the long process of my body purging everything I had eaten in the last 24 hours. I took every
arsenal in my medicine cabinet designed to fight the
vomiting monster, but nothing really helped. At
11:00 am, I realized that I must be running a fever
(which I was) and so called my oncologist who
ordered me to come in. My parents had to come
and get me as I could not even hold my head up at
this point. At the oncologist's office, it was the
conclusion of my doctor and of yours truly that I
was suffering from food poisoning. *Don't ask.*
(Okay, okay, I ate something for lunch on Sunday
that had been in my fridge a little too long.) Please,
no messages that say, "You shouldn't do that!" I've
heard that from everyone here including myself.

The oncologist ordered a CBC which showed all my
blood levels are normal! Yeah!!! This was just a
good, old fashioned case of food poisoning. So, at
his office in the chemo chair, I got fluids, another
anti-nausea med, and an antibiotic, just to make
sure the food poisoning didn't turn into infection.
After sitting there for over 3 hours and trying to
sleep, I was so ready to get home! Once home I
think I slept for 4 or 5 hours straight. Once my
stomach would allow more than just a sip of water,
I was able to get down some Tylenol which then
helped with the aches and pains. By Tuesday morning I felt like a completely different person!

So I was able to get my Herceptin yesterday without consequence. I am feeling quite good now and
gearing up for next week's chemo.

May 26, 2009 10:16 PM, CDT

I am ready for my chemo tomorrow. I'm a little nervous about how I will feel afterwards. After my last chemo on that Wednesday, I was so hungry for something sweet that I rushed home and made oatmeal cookies. They tasted really good at the time. But now, remembering how I felt that evening, I can't *stand* the thought of oatmeal cookies!

We had a really nice little road trip to Mineola, TX on Saturday. We left here about noon. Grabbed lunch on the way. Stopped at a couple of historical markers and old cemeteries. Took a couple of detours down one lane roads. Then we walked around the old downtown of Mineola and let the kids explore the old caboose that sits near the new Amtrak station. Finally, we got dinner at the East Texas Burger Company and ate it out on the gazebo. They have tables and chairs set up out there. We were the only ones out there, so it was really nice. We all had a nice time. The kids were very well behaved. Then we drove on home and got to sleep in our own beds. Heaven! I must say that my sweet husband totally redeemed himself with that trip! And it did wonders for my spirit.

At church, we are still on Ephesians. This Sunday, Pete followed Paul's example and prayed that we would not just invite Jesus in as a guest, but that we would have Him as an active participant in every aspect of our lives. As I listened, I felt a strong spirit of conviction. I got real prompting from the Holy Spirit telling me that I have been living my life in public one way, but in the privacy of my own home, I have *not* asked Jesus to truly participate in my life—not in my relationship with my kids and not in my marriage. It was a real wake up call for me! I won't make promises that I can't keep. All I can do is try to pray more often and make the effort to allow the Holy Spirit to make the decisions around here. I have done a better job over the last 2 days, but I still have a ways to go. Pray for me! :-) But please, pray that I "get it" *without* something bad happening to make me "get it." I've had enough of that!

On my knees with palms up,
Tracy

May 30, 2009 11:30 AM, CDT

Chemo Wednesday has come and gone. I felt yucky on Wednesday night but not nearly as bad as last time. I took my Emends for nausea on Thursday and Friday. I also took Zofran for the same issue. I got my Neulasta on Thursday and am feeling the effects of it now. I feel as if I have had a very vigorous workout. Every muscle in my body is sore. The only problem here is that I won't reap any *obvious* physical benefits. I say obvious because I will reap the benefit of having my white blood cell count staying up in the safe range. That is pretty important!

I'm looking forward to the summer and the many activities planned. We will be busy, but at least I will have Rafe home with me for a little while.

11

June 2009 was more of the same, except that I had Rafe and the kids home with me.

> *June 1, 2009 11:10 AM, CDT*

I felt better yesterday. My sore muscles were no longer sore. But the tiredness remains. My husband was kind. He held down the fort while I got a 2 hour nap. I woke up still tired but better.

I am feeling almost my "normal" self again—whatever that is!

Thank you, my friends and family! I love you all.

Tracy

> *June 3, 2009 9:52 PM, CDT*

I have good news to report. I saw my oncologist today. He told me that I only have 2 more treatments left. Originally, he had said, I would have FEC every 3 weeks for 4 months, but apparently he meant for 4 treatments. So, that means I will be ready for surgery the end of July and/or the first of August. As much as I am dreading the surgery, I am excited to get this phase of my life over with.

I already have an appointment with a plastic surgeon next Thursday. He is the same plastic surgeon I met a while back at the FORCE Meeting (support group for women with hereditary cancer). My surgeon, Dr. Anglin, also spoke at that meeting and she has recommended him. He seems pretty knowledgeable, but I will know more after I meet with him.

More good news—my hair has already started to grow back in. I never lost is completely. It had just gotten really thin in spots and bald in some spots. During my week without chemo, it started to come back in and continues to grow. I have been worried that it would fall out again with the new chemo drug, but my doctor told me today it probably won't. Now if I can just get it to thicken up a little more, I will quit wearing my wigs. I had a dream last night that it had all grown back! What a great dream!

God bless!

June 12, 2009 8:38 PM, CDT

On Wednesday I got my weekly Herceptin (the antibody). Then on Wednesday night, Jenni Keith (Aunt Jenni who set up this caring bridge site for me) and I went out to dinner in Coppell. We knew storms were coming, but we never imagined that about half way through our meal we would be huddled up with strangers in the back hallway of the very dark restaurant. The lights went off about the same time that the tornado sirens started. Such fun!

I saw the plastic surgeon on Thursday. What an embarrassing situation that is!!! I would *never* volunteer to go through that! Basically, pictures are taken and measurements are made while you have to stand there in your birthday suit. All I can say is after having suffered through that—my new breasts better look great.

He told me that he will put in the spacers immediately after Dr. Anglin, my surgeon, completes the mastectomy. Those will be slowly inflated with water every 2 weeks for 6 weeks. Then, if I need to have radiation, that will take 6 weeks. Then I will have to wait 6 weeks before they can do the reconstruction surgery. I added that up on the calendar and figure that with any luck, I can get both surgeries in before the end of the year. I would like to get it done under the same insurance year since we've already paid our full deductible and met our total out of pocket for the year.

June 14, 2009 4:06 PM, CDT

Chemo this week. Pray for me! :-) And pray for Rafe!

June 20, 2009 1:14 PM, CDT

I'm trying very hard to swallow a few bites of lunch today. This has been a rough one. Between the chemo—just wish I could throw up and feel better—tummy issues and the Neulasta—every muscle in my body feels like I have been beaten up by a professional boxer—I am really feeling the effects this time. I am so glad I only have to do this one more time, because I just can't imagine having to go through much more of this. This time has been much worse than the last 2. Even thinking about doing this again in 3 weeks makes me sick to my stomach.

June 22, 2009 12:10 PM, CDT

I'm finally feeling better today. I felt a little better last night. Ate a rib and some potato salad and beans yesterday at my mom and dad's house. Yum. Also some fresh, home grown tomatoes. Then had a sandwich last night with those same tomatoes.

This morning, I woke up feeling sooo much better and craving a chicken fried steak. So I convinced Rafe to take me to Pete's Cafe here in Carrollton. I ate the whole steak! Sooo good. Rafe said, "Wow, you were hungry!" Yes, I was!

I am up and moving and feeling better all around. Still tired, but I'll take tired.

We have less than 2 weeks until our trip to Joni and Friends Family Retreat. Can't wait!!! I'm preparing my lists of what to take. So much to do.

I am going without any wig or head wrap today. I even dropped Hope off at her summer school this morning sans head wrap. Feels good to be me — even if people do look at me like, "Lady, what were you thinking cutting your hair that short?"

June 23, 2009 8:55 PM, CDT

I saw my oncologist today. My white blood cell counts are good. (I hate the way Neulasta makes me feel, but I am thankful that it does its job.) My hemoglobin is on the low side at 10.2 which is why I am so tired. They can give me Procrit, but my insurance won't pay for it until my hemoglobin count is under 10. So, Doc says I'll just have to be tired. He did say I am also low in iron again, so he will give me some iron next week which will also help.

My next chemo treatment is July 8th. I will continue with the weekly Herceptin treatment until July 29th. That marks 6 months on it. After that, I will get the Herceptin every 3 weeks until the one year mark which is in January. Herceptin can be hard on your heart which is why they give a smaller dose once a week when you are on chemo. Once I am no longer receiving chemo, I can then get the larger dose every 3 weeks. Make sense?

He said I am clear for surgery the first week of August. I will see my surgeon on Monday to discuss that. And he looked for the tumor again today but could *not* feel anything!!! Praise and glory be to God!!! I know I still have a long road ahead of me, but He who led me here will lead me out!!!

June 25, 2009 11:32 AM, CDT

Rafe and I just had an argument that at the time just made me angry. Later, when I had a chance to cool off and think of things from his point of view, I realized that he is *terrified* that something will happen to me and he will be left to care for Hope and Walker on his own. He is especially concerned about being able to earn a living and care for Walker as he ages. It absolutely breaks my heart that he has this weight on his shoulders.

12

July is usually our favorite month of the year because it is the month we attend Joni and Friends Family Retreat for families dealing with a disability. July 2009 was no different except that year I had very little hair. Still, we had a wonderful time and enjoyed our respite from all things related to cancer. When we returned home, I went back for my very last chemo, and then the preparations for surgery began.

July 1, 2009 10:48 PM, CDT

I saw my surgeon on Monday. My surgery is tentatively scheduled for August 12th. I am to see another surgeon about having my ovaries removed on the same day. I will see him next Thursday. Of course, I am having chemo on Wednesday, so I just hope I feel well enough to visit with that new doctor.

So, I will have surgery on August 12th at which time I will have my double mastectomy and also my ovaries removed (oophorectomy). On that same date, the plastic surgeon will come in and place spacers in the area that will become my new breasts.

I will have to wait 6 weeks before having radiation. Then radiation will take approx 6 weeks. Then I will have to wait another 6 weeks before I can have my reconstruction surgery which will hopefully be in December '09.

It took longer than expect today to get my weekly Herceptin because I forgot they also had to give me some iron and that takes an hour and a half. Rafe and Walker came up to bring me some lunch. Walker was so funny. First, he ate all of my fries. But then, he was so glad to see me that he sat in the lounger with me. Then he didn't want to leave. I wonder what he thought I was there for!

July 8, 2009 12:56 PM, CDT

We are back from Joni and Friends Family Retreat for people with special needs and their families and sadly, back to the real world. I say that because JAF is so far removed from the real world that we often say it is the closest thing to heaven here on earth. I have lots of wonderful stories to share with all of you and some pictures to post as well. I will do that as soon as possible.

I was scheduled to get my last chemo today, however, it seems God had other plans. I am neutropenic, meaning my neutrophils are too low. I was given a Neupogen shot and told to come back tomorrow. I also have an appointment with Dr. Oh tomorrow (the doctor who is to remove my ovaries). I am not sure how I am going to fit all of that in. I need to hurry and figure something out before the end of the day today.

July 10, 2009 3:52 PM, CDT

Hi all,

I just wanted to let you all know that I did have chemo yesterday, and I'm feeling really well today! Praise God! I was shaky, and hungover feeling (sorry but there is no other way to describe it) last night but still managed to go up to our Special Needs support group at church. I am so glad that I did since my friends always make me laugh and laughter is the best medicine.

I went to get my Neulasta shot today and my iron as well. I am feeling surprising well and have even eaten some lunch today. (I ate cheese and crackers last night.) Last treatment, I was nauseous the entire time and only ate soup for about 5 days. I am soooo thankful to the Lord for helping me to feel so great today! And thank you Lord for really good pharmaceuticals!!!

Let me say that Rafe and I are sooo very thankful for every single meal we have received (including gift cards).

July 14, 2009 6:55 PM, CDT

I did really well over the weekend. I was tired, achy, and sore, but I had none of the nausea that I experienced 3 weeks earlier.

I took 2 naps yesterday and then fell asleep early last night (early for our house). I then woke up this morning around 4:00 am with Hope and felt really run-down and yucky. I felt the same at 5:00 when Rafe and I heard Walker crying. Thank you, Rafe, for getting up with him. And I felt the same at 7:30. Rafe had to get Walker on the bus for summer school and then he had to get Hope dressed and off to her VBS. I just couldn't make it. I finally woke up around 10:30. I drank some coffee and felt like eating a piece of toast. I finally checked my temp around 12:30 and found that it was 99.6. I am supposed to call the doctor if it gets above 100.4. I took some Tylenol and finally felt a little better this afternoon. I'm not really sure what is going on.

And, to top things off, my hair appears to be thinning again. I noticed it yesterday when I got my hair wet. I refuse to wash it again (like that is going to keep it from going). Rafe brushed off the back of my shirt this afternoon and said, "You're right, it is falling out." *Bummer!*

July 15, 2009 2:30 PM, CDT

Just got home from the doctors. I was scheduled for my weekly Herceptin. They checked my blood and it turns out, I am extremely neutropenic, meaning my white blood cell counts are next to nothing. Makes me very susceptible to infection. So, I was *not* given my Herceptin but instead given a Neupogen shot and a script for an antibiotic and sent home. I will go back tomorrow for another Neupogen shot and then go in on Friday for my Herceptin. Rafe asked me if all of this is normal for chemo. I replied that I don't think there is a "normal" for chemo. There are no rules here.

July 17, 2009 4:03 PM, CDT

I went back to the oncologist's office again today to

get my Herceptin, but after 2 Neupogen shots and horrible bone pain, my neutrophils are still too low. My white blood cell count is up, but my neutrophils have to be at least 2 and they are still just 4. See Neutrophil definition below.

> **Neutrophil:** A type of white blood cell, specifically a form of granulocyte, filled with neutrally-staining granules, tiny sacs of enzymes that help the cell to kill and digest microorganisms it has engulfed by phagocytosis. The mature neutrophil has a segmented nucleus (it is called a seg or poly) while the immature neutrophil has band-shape nucleus (it is called a band). The neutrophil has a lifespan of about 3 days.

> **Neutropenia,** a decreased proportion of neutrophils, may be seen with viral infections and after radiotherapy and chemotherapy. Neutropenia lowers the immunologic barrier to bacterial and fungal infection.

So, I was given my 3rd Neupogen shot for the week and sent home. We will see next week what my counts are like and whether I can get my Herceptin. I'm a little worried about what *not* getting my weekly Herceptin this week means, but I will just have to hand it all over to my doctor and to the Lord.

My doctor is still out of town on vacation. He will be back to work next week, so I will see on Monday what he wants to do. Luckily, my Lord never goes on vacation!

With all of this bone pain, I was *not* happy to see the nurse pull out that Neupogen shot. She cautiously laid it out on the table and was afraid to show it to me. She knew I was not going to be happy! Oh well, how much worse can the pain get, right? Scratch that!!! I don't want to know. She did give me permission to take a little ibuprofen for the pain (usually you can only take Tylenol) since my other blood counts are good. Tylenol just doesn't cut it with this. I can take Vicodin, but I don't have the kind of life where I can just go to bed. On that note, while Hope is taking a nap, I think I will go stretch out on my bed with Walker. I wonder if he'll let me watch something other than Pokémon.

July 19, 2009 11:07 PM, CDT

I am feeling so much better!! All I can figure out is that I must have been trying to come down with some kind of bacterial infection while my white blood cell counts were low. All of the Neupogen shots and the Levaquin (an antibiotic) must have done the trick, because I feel like a real person again. I even got hungry today (something I hadn't experienced in a week).

As my surgery date draws nearer, I get more and more afraid. I am trying to hand it all over to the Lord. Pray for me on that matter. As I finish my chemo treatments, I am praying that I am done with cancer forever. I worry because for every woman I meet who tells me they or someone they know had breast cancer and has been cancer free for 5, 10, 15, or more years, I meet another woman who is going through it again. I met a woman at chemo who had it 12 years ago, battled and won it then, but it has now gone into her lungs and bones and is considered stage 4. Twelve years is not long enough for me! I have a 4 year old daughter!!! She will still need me at 16!!! I am 42 and still need to speak to my mom almost every day!

At church today, the choir sang a song about our being salt and light to this world. That is our job. So I'm thinking, well then, I need to stay here a lot longer.

Our regular pastor was out of town, so the guest pastor Mark told a hilarious story about his teenage son borrowing his prized guitar. He said he would never let his son play that guitar but finally relented with 15 million rules attached. One night, his son forgot those rules and took it with him while he walked across the street to speak to the neighbor. He then slipped on the wet sidewalk and fell down on top of the guitar. Mark said he heard his son screaming from outside and thought, "Oh no! My son has been shot or hit or both!" So he rushes outside and meets his son at the door. His son is crying and almost hyperventilating and finally says, "Dad, I fell on your guitar!" Mark said he looked at his son and thought, "Why couldn't you have been shot?" Of course, he didn't say that but instead said, "Son, it's just a guitar. I love you a lot more than I love that guitar." That reminded me of the thousands of things of mine that Walker has broken over the years. I thought about the bite marks on the inside of the doors of my car and pictures he has taken off the walls. I have cried out, "Why can't I have *anything nice*?" But the truth is, I love Walker a lot more than I like nice things. Mark is right. Those are just things and we should never value them more than people. I am thankful to Walker for teaching me that.

Mark told that story to illustrate his last point that when you know someone who is going through a mess, you should be willing to give them or loan them things that are important to you. When he made that point, I looked over at Rafe and asked, "Who do we know here at Bent Tree who owns a Cadillac?" We might just need to borrow it! :-)

July 22, 2009 1:25 PM, CDT

On Monday, my doctor's office called and told me to come in to get my Herceptin. While I was there they checked my blood counts as usual. My white blood cell count was 30(reference is around 11, I believe)! That last Neupogen shot really worked! So, I got a double dose of my Herceptin since I missed it last week. I did fine with that with no reactions, thank goodness. I also got my 3rd echo-cardiogram. No news yet on how that went.

He also said that I don't need to get the Benadryl every time, if I don't want it. I hate the way the Benadryl makes me feel for the rest of the day, so I would prefer not to have it if possible. I did get it this week just because of the increased dose.

I am really tired today and don't have much of an appetite. The good news there is that I actually lost about 5 lbs in the last 2 weeks. Yeah! Bad way to lose weight, but I'm still happy.

Only 3 more weekends before my surgery. Oh boy.

13

The month of August was surgery month. I had a double mastectomy and an oophorectomy, which is the fancy term for having your ovaries removed. Our wonderful friends from church arranged a "While You Were Out" project for our home during this month. They did so much in such a short time!

August is my son's birth month which is always emotional for me. Dealing with cancer only added to that.

God's presence was strongly felt this month!

August 2, 2009 11:17 PM, CDT

Sorry it has been so long since my last update.

I had my Herceptin on Wednesday. I got the full dose and don't have to get another until August 26th! I am soooo happy about that. I was Neutropenic again, but the Doc said I would bounce back on my own and wouldn't need another shot. He does want me to come in on the 10th to have my blood tested one more time before my surgery. That way, if it is low, they can give me a shot to raise my wbc count up before surgery.

Okay, so for a quick update, I go in for Pre op testing (whatever that is) on August 7th (Friday). Then on Monday, I go over to the plastic surgeon's office so that he can mark where he wants the incisions. Then, that afternoon, I will go over to my oncologist's office so that he can check my blood counts again. Finally, my surgery will be on August 12th.

August 5, 2009 10:32 AM, CDT

Today is Walker's 15th birthday! When Walker was a little baby, I would tell him, "Walker, tell Momma a story!" Fifteen years later, I am still waiting for that story. I stand firm in my faith that one day I will get that story!!! Come on, Walker, tell Momma a story!!! (Thank you, Jesus!)

We are going to take Walker and Hope on the DART rail today for Walker's birthday. It is difficult to find things he enjoys. I am pretty sure he will like this. Then on Friday (they don't run on Wednesdays) we will take him on the Tarantula Train in Ft. Worth. It is an old steam locomotive.

Happy Birthday, Walker-boy!!! I love you!

August 7, 2009 1:34 PM, CDT

Had my pre op testing today. My surgery is set. Wednesday Aug. 12th @ Medical Center of Plano. The actual surgery is at 10:00am. I have to be there by 7:00. First they will do a Sentinel Node biopsy to determine which of my lymph nodes need to come out. Then they will take me to surgery. The surgery will last anywhere from 5 to 7 hours more or less. Am I nervous? Yes.

I will post more later.

August 9, 2009 2:55 PM, CDT

Many people have asked what they can do for us over the next couple of weeks. I will tell you....

1. Pray!!! Pray that all goes right during my surgery and that nothing goes wrong. Pray for wisdom and expertise for my Doctors. Pray for strength for my husband, my parents, and sisters, and brothers-in-law, etc. Pray for peace for my children!! Most of all pray that Jesus keeps His wonderful and merciful hand on Walker and Hope the entire time!!! (Especially Walker since he is not in school this week and is going to be spending a lot of time with his attendant.) Please pray that Ms. Tonja has the strength and fortitude she needs this week!

2. Because I cannot drive over the next couple of weeks—groceries would be a blessing to us. I am going to post a list of some staples for us. I will post this need on my care calendar so that someone can sign up for it, however, if you just find yourself in the car with an extra bottle of ketchup for Walker please fill free to come on by! :-)

3. I have posted meals on my calendar, but left off the days while I am in the hospital—no sense in bringing a meal over when we won't be here. However, someone asked about the kids and gift cards. Walker and Hope love the typical food places—Whataburger (Walker's favorite), McDonalds, KFC, even Church's Fried Chicken would all be great places for gift cards.

Thank you! Thank you!! Thank you!!! I can't express how much your love, concern, prayers, etc. means to our family!!!

Love to all!!!

Tracy

August 11, 2009 3:47 PM, CDT

This is my last post before my surgery. I will try to remind Rafe to come on and update everyone, but who knows. I will post again as soon as I am able to sit up straight and type!

First, thanks again for all of the prayers!!! Thanks also for the love, the hugs, the well-wishes, the cards, the dinners, the money, the time, etc., etc. We are sooo incredibly thankful!

I went to see the plastic surgeon yesterday to have him draw lines on me for the surgeon. The funny thing is that the very first mark on the base of my neck is in the shape of a cross. I am well covered.

I am to report to the hospital tomorrow morning at 7:00 am. As soon as I arrive at the hospital they will take me down to mammography where they will do a Sentinel Node biopsy. They will inject some radioactive liquid into my lymph nodes and see where it goes. They wait 1 hour and then take pictures. Then the surgeon will know just how many lymph nodes need to come out.

Once they have done that, they will take me to surgery. The surgery will last anywhere from 5 to 7 hours. Hopefully no more!

To answer some questions, I am not sure they will allow me to take my prayer blankets into surgery, but I will ask and even if not, I will have them with me for my mom to cover me up as soon as I come out.

The hospital has given me a small pillow to put on my chest while in the car and just to apply pressure. I will also use this to deflect Walker from knocking into me. I'm pretty good at doing that anyway!

I wore my "Got Chemo" shirt today (mostly because it is the only shirt I own that covers up my doctor marks) to both our Bible Study (Love you, Ladies!) and to my oncologists office. I had to get my blood checked again today just to make sure that my blood counts were good and that I didn't need Neupogen. They were and I didn't, Praise God! Anyway, I have worn that shirt many times before, but today so many people noticed it and commented on it! I told them that I plan on retiring this shirt and going back to Survivor Gals where I bought it and will purchase the "Survivor" shirt next!

Lastly, please pray but do not worry. I am in the hands of a great surgeon and, most importantly, in the hands of the Great Physician!!! I know that He will be with me and is fighting this battle for me. I also know that He made me really stubborn for a reason!!! He will lead me out of this mess just like he has so many others! I'll talk to all of you soon!

Love you all!

Tracy

August 18, 2009 10:30 PM, CDT

Dearest Family and Friends,

Well, I am alive and kicking. I have been through, well, not sure how many rounds with the alien, but I *am alive* and it *is not!* God is the victor—*now and forever*.

I have much to share, but as I am on many, many meds, and it has been a long day, I need to make this short. I have been home from the hospital since Sunday night. All prayers about my staying longer than the 1 night originally scheduled were answered very loudly by God. He said more than *yes!* He answered *sooo* many other prayers that I am very anxious to share with all of you when I can. (Let me just say that my faith is *much* stronger now than it was even last week at this time.) Just know that *He* is King and He is sitting gloriously on His throne tonight. I love Him and I love all of you!!!

August 23, 2009 5:11 PM, CDT

I had a very long message written but my computer froze and the message vanished. I can only assume that it was *not* the message God wanted me to post. *So....*

All went well during my 7 hour surgery on August 12th. Dr. Oh, the gynecological oncologist went first. His part only took approx 15 to 20 minutes. He removed my ovaries and tubes laparoscopically. (Very little pain.) Then Dr. Anglin did her part, followed my Dr. Meade, the very handsome (and *young*) plastic surgeon. All went well.

The following day, I developed a hematoma (internal bleeding) in my left breast and had to be rushed to emergency surgery that night. I was really worried as I had not been breathing very well anyway (due to being intubated on the previous day's surgery), and the way I was breathing so shallowly due to the pain in my chest and the morphine. I was so afraid I would come down with pneumonia or that something else would go wrong during that surgery. So, I prayed. I prayed that God would spare my life, that He wouldn't take my kids' mom and my husband's wife away. I prayed that He would rescue me this time just as He has many other times. And He answered *yes*. I felt the answer just before I went into surgery. Then I felt it again when I woke up. There is *no* doubt in my mind that *He* was with me during that surgery and the hours following.

I had lost a pint of blood and the doctor had prepared for me to receive a blood transfusion the next morning. He told my sister that the way my kidney's functioned during the night would determine whether I needed that transfusion. I am happy to report that I had to get up 4 or 5 times during the night (had to call the nurse each time to help me up) to go to the restroom. By 7:00 am, Dr. Meade came by to tell me that he had cancelled the transfusion. *Yeah God!!!* If I could have gotten up on that bed and danced that day, I would have! I know my heart was dancing!

I just want all of you to know that while I talk (or type) a lot about my faith, there are many times (like the week before my surgery) when my faith is very weak. I have spent way too many hours wondering if I can really count on God. My week in the hospital reassured me a hundred times over and has restored my faith immeasurably!!! Having cancer sucks! But feeling God sitting next to you on a hospital bed is an *amazing* feeling!!!

And wait till I tell you all about what our friends from Bent Tree Bible have done for us! That will have to wait. Hope is home from swimming and is hungry.

Love to all!

Tracy

August 26, 2009 9:19 PM, CDT

I saw my oncologist today. My friend Mary volunteered to drop me off at the doctors since I still can't drive and to keep Hope this afternoon. I really do have the best friends in the entire world.

I had my Herceptin, but my red blood cell count was low due to the blood loss in the hospital. So I finally got a Procrit shot. I got it in my belly! :-) I know some of you are getting dizzy just thinking about that.

My doctor agreed that I seem to have another little hematoma (bleed) on the right breast this time. It is small and should heal on its own. It is just painful as heck. It is beginning to feel better.

Doctor also prescribed some kind of medicine that should *kill* every bit of hormone production in my body. Even though my ovaries are gone, they want to make sure I don't have any more hormones circling around trying to make cancer. He said he doesn't like to see cancer in anyone but *especially* not in a young woman like me. Thank you, Dr. Saez!

On the other hand, it finally happened. I knew it would someday, but today was the day. The lady who helps monitor the kids on Walker's bus asked me if Hope was my grandbaby!!! I just laughed and said, "*No*, she's mine."

It is not unreasonable for her to think that. I am 42 and have a 15 year old who started high school this week. *Yes*, that's right! My baby boy is now going to high school. And he still loves to cuddle up in bed with mom. I really wish he would be embarrassed by that! :-) He is so funny! I know he is happy to be back in school.

August 29, 2009 11:58 AM, CDT

Went to see the Nurse Practitioner at my surgeon's office yesterday to have the 2 remaining drains removed. What a day! First, Hope and I were getting in the car to head over there at 1:00 — for 1:30 appt time — when I noticed a message on my cell phone. It was from the Nurse Practitioner stating that she needed to change our appt time to 2:30. I already had Hope dressed and in the car, so there was no way I was going to get her out and wait another hour before heading that way. So, I called the doctor's office and was put on hold for about 10 minutes while Hope and I drove around. I finally hung up and called to make sure that Walker's attendant would be at the house by 3:00 to get Walker off the bus. Found out then that her son has the flu. So, I then had to call my mom and dad to see if they could get Walker off the bus. They could, thank goodness, so then I tried to call the school transportation to let the bus driver know that my parents would be getting Walker off the bus. I was afraid that they wouldn't release him to them since our current bus driver has not met my parents yet. Never could get anyone at transportation to answer the phone Then Hope and I decided to pull into Dairy Queen to get a drink. Ordered and then realized I did not have my wallet. So, we then had to drive home to get my wallet and then back to DQ.

We finally arrived at the doctor's office and saw the Nurse practitioner. She did not want to remove my drains because she had not gotten word from the Plastic surgeon that it was okay to remove said drains. But when I saw the plastic surgeon he never mentioned that I needed to continue calling in my numbers. He only said that yes Dr. Anglin's office could remove the drains as long as they knew the numbers needed to be below 30 (which they were). In fact, I had cancelled an appointment for earlier in the week because the numbers were still too high. So, Debra, the Nurse practitioner went to call Dr. Meade and spoke with his nurse who gave the okay for her to remove the drains.

Then I mentioned the hematoma! Oh boy!!! She then proceeded to gripe at me for not immediately calling Dr. Meade (the plastic surgeon) to be seen about it. She made me promise to make an ap-pointment to see Dr. Meade by Monday morning. She also asked if I had been using my arms a lot. I told her that no, I had been careful, but that I could not just sit around and keep my arms at my sides for weeks on end. I have 2 kids and responsibilities, for goodness sakes! Also, Dr. Meade had told me not to be afraid to use my arms! Needless to say, I wasn't very happy with Debra.

I was hoping that once I got those drains removed I would feel much better, but I have to say "no". I'm still in pain and I still couldn't sleep on my side last night. And my back hurts when I sleep on my back. So, I was still quite miserable last night. I got up at 8:30 this morning and finally took another Vicodin.

To top it all off, Walker was in a good mood when he got up this morning, but then for some reason got really cranky. Boy!!! Sorry for the vent, but I feel better now!

August 31, 2009 8:28 PM, CDT

I ran a fever this weekend 100.2. I called the doctor on call for my plastic surgeon. He took down the information and said he would text my plastic surgeon. Since I already had an appointment today, I wasn't surprised when Dr. Meade did not call me back. The fever disappeared during the afternoon and came back up late last night. It was gone this morning.

Today during my appointment with my plastic surgeon, he said the doctor on call had told him I was running a fever and had flu like symptoms. *At no time* did I ever tell that doctor that I had flu like symptoms. He asked me if I had any other symptoms and I said, "No, I just feel yucky like you do when you have a fever."

At any rate, Dr. Meade said that if I run a fever anymore, regardless of my symptoms, he will put me on antibiotics. Nothing is red, so he said I shouldn't worry about it. Everything looks good including the hematoma which he said I should press in with my thumb and it will go away. (I'm not kidding. He really said that!) He also said I could start to do some range-of-motion and light stretching exercises. *Yes!* I go back in 2 months to get my expanders expanded a little more.

I actually do feel a little better (a little). I was even able to sleep on my side last night for 5 minutes at a time. I also figured out that if I put a pillow under my knees while I am sleeping on my back, my lower back doesn't hurt.

The painter is coming tomorrow to paint Walker's room and the new doors and trim in the hall way. I haven't really discussed this—this was all initiated by some ladies from my church and my Bible study. This was a "while you were out" project they did while I was in the hospital.

Praying God's blessings on all of you!

Love,
Tracy

14

September of 2009 was a month of healing, physically and spiritually, and was the beginning of my radiation. There was so much on my mind that month as I finally began to come out of the fog created by surgery and pain meds.

September 2, 2009 9:38 AM, CDT

Nothing new to report. I'm still having an issue with pain in that right breast caused by that hematoma. It is especially painful late in the evening. Feels like someone is shoving a golf ball into my chest as hard as they can *all the time! Ouch!!* I think my husband thinks I'm faking!

September 6, 2009 3:51 PM, CDT

I saw the doctor in charge of my radiation (Radiologist? That doesn't sound right.) on Thursday. I have until this coming Thursday to get my left arm flexible enough to hold up over my head so that they can do a CT scan and get me positioned correctly for radiation. Then I will start radiation the following week. They will radiate the lymph nodes in my left shoulder (just above the breast), the left breast, and the nodes under my arm (the ones not removed during surgery). The goal is to zap any stray cells and keep them from popping up. I don't believe there are any, but you just can't be too careful where cancer is concerned. I like being cancer free!!!

The good news is that I was able to get both of my arms up today to praise and worship the Lord! Awesome!!!

Our Pastor at church was back after his summer sabbatical. He had much to share. One thing that popped into my mind this morning that I will share concerns Hope—my daughter, not the feeling. During this cancer scare, I have been most concerned for her. I know without a shadow of a doubt that Walker will go to heaven. Hope has the gift/curse of free will. She will have to make a choice. I have been very concerned that if I did not survive this thing, that she would be left here to deal with her brother and her dad and might become bitter and turn away from God. I can't help but feel that she needs me here more than Rafe and Walker combined. *However*, in the last couple of days, while Hope and I have been reading from her children's Bible, she has been asking me all sorts of questions that I'm not sure I have answers to.

Today, sitting in church, it hit me. She is God's— either to save or not to save. All I can do is to help steer her on the right course, but the decision is ultimately hers and only God knows which she will choose. I am praying that I am here to witness her make the *right* choice, but again, that is up to God. That thought actually gives me a lot of peace.

Pete also talked about trusting God I have no doubts that God loves me, but I still have issues with trust. The reason is that what is in my best interest does not always equal what I want. Hard for me to reconcile the two. For example, right now it is in my daughter's best interest to be punished and sent to her room. You can trust me, she's not going to like it!

Current day note: Hope asked Jesus to be her Savior in the summer of 2011 during vacation Bible school. Then on November 24, 2013, she was baptized in our church.

September 8, 2009 10:01 AM, CDT

I was feeling really great until Sunday night into Monday. For some reason, my left arm and armpit feel swollen and have begun to throb terribly. I hadn't taken any Vicodin in about a week but had to take 2 yesterday and 1 this morning at 5:00 am.

I called my doctor this morning. He wants me to come in to see him tomorrow morning (he is in surgery all day today). He has instructed me to stay on my pain meds and limit my arm movement. I told him that I have been trying to stretch that muscle to be ready to get fitted for the radiation table this Thursday. But I will rest it until I see him tomorrow. He was going to refill my antibiotic but decided to see me tomorrow and then make that decision. I am to call him immediately if I run a fever or if the pain gets worse.

I can't help but feel like this is a setback. I was feeling so great!!! I guess maybe I tried to push it a little too fast. Also, when I was at the doctor's office last week, I forgot to tell the nurse to take my blood pressure on my right side. Because I had those lymph nodes removed on the left, I am *never* supposed to have my blood pressure checked on that side. My nurses at the oncologist's office have been making me practice this for the last 6 months and of course, while in the hospital, they actually took it on my legs. But on my first real test, I failed miserably! Thankfully, it hurt when the cuff began to inflate and then I realized it and yanked it off. (The nurse is supposed to ask and forgot as well.) I just can't help but wonder if that contributed to my problem in some way. I don't think I'll ever forget again!!!

I know my last posting sounded a little negative. That was the state I was in, but I want to assure all of you that I know how much God loves me, because of the way He has taken care of us in the last 6 months through all of you!!! In fact, all I have to do is look at our checking account. It may sound funny, but if you had told me 6 months ago that through all of this, our bank account would have remained solvent this year, I would never have believed it! Rafe and I were talking about this and he said that is because we've had so many people help us out with either money or gift cards or both. I said, *yes*, that is the way God works! He blesses people by using them to bless others. He is so awesome!

Vicodin kicking in so I will close.

Love to you all!

September 9, 2009 2:36 PM, CDT

I ran a fever last night (100.9). I took Tylenol and it went away and did not come back this morning. I saw the plastic surgeon about it this morning. He said it looks good and he does not want to put me on any antibiotics unless I absolutely have to have them. I am to let him know if I run a fever again.

While I was there, I discussed reconstruction with him again. I learned some things today that make me rethink my plan. I will post this information later. Rafe and I are still discussing it and haven't made a decision yet as to which way to go. Please pray for wisdom for us and for my doctor.

I have an appt with the radiation doctor tomorrow. I tried to reschedule it, but the nurse said in light of my pain, the doctor wants to see me tomorrow anyway and we will plan. I'll let you know what he has to say.

September 13, 2009 8:17 PM, CDT

I start radiation on Wednesday, September 16th. I will have 25 consecutive treatments every day of the week except Saturdays and Sundays. When I saw the doc on Thursday, they had me lay on a table with my arms up over my head. They made a form that will put me in to make sure I am in the correct position. They then made some marks on me with a permanent marker which they then covered up with some really good tape. They then ran me through the CAT scan machine. On Wednesday, they will remove the tape and then put tiny tattoos on me as placement markers.

I was instructed to continue to stretch that left arm out. I have done so for the last couple of days and now seem to be suffering from the same ailment as last weekend minus the throbbing. My armpit is extremely tender and sore and, can you believe it, I am running another slight fever.

September 16, 2009 1:42 PM, CDT

I got my first dose of radiation today. I was supposed to also get my Herceptin, but they were so busy that there was *no* way we could get finished with that before I was to pick Hope up today at 2:00. I even went to the oncologist's before going to radiation so that they could do my blood draw and run my CBC first just to get it out of the way. Luckily the radiation place and my oncologist's office are in the same building. I will have to go back and get that done on Friday morning before my radiation appt.

The radiation wasn't horrible. It took longer today than it normally will because they had to make sure I was in the exact right location, take xrays to be sure, and also deliver treatment. I was so nervous that I tensed up my foot and my arms, then I couldn't move them first for over 10 minutes, then after about a 3 minute break, another 10 minutes. By the time we were finished, my left arm was totally asleep! From now on, it should only take a few minutes each day. And you can't even tell that you are being microwaved. The only clue is the beeping and buzzing of the machine when it kicks on and off.

Thursday, September 24, 2009 3:54 PM, CDT

All is well with radiation. I am 7 treatments in. I have 18 more to go.

15

October of 2009 was proof that God can take you straight through the fire and back out again. I didn't exactly come out unscathed from the radiation— burns and blisters under my left arm and what can only be described as a "sunburn" of sorts on my left shoulder. I also began having lymphedema in that left arm. I would learn later that it was most likely from the radiation done to the remaining lymph nodes on that side. What doesn't kill you makes you stronger, and also gives you strange side effects for the rest of your life.

October 12, 2009 6:33 PM, CDT

Sorry for the long span between updates. No excuse—just lazy!

I developed a rash on my chest that could not be explained by the radiation as it was on both sides. The itching was really getting to me, so my oncologist prescribed methylprednisolone, a steroid, in a taper pack. I finished up the last dose last night. Now I am afraid it will come back. I am praying that it won't.

The H1N1 has made an appearance at our house. Hope developed a cough on Friday and then a high fever early Saturday morning. Luckily her doctor is open on Saturday mornings. He did a flu test and confirmed that she had H1N1. He immediately started her on Tamiflu and warned me to watch for any signs of infection. She has not run a fever since Sunday morning. If she continues to do well tonight, she'll be going to school tomorrow. (Yippee.)

After leaving the pediatrician's office on Saturday, I called Walker's doctor who sent Tamiflu for him to begin right away. Because of his autism, he is in the at risk category. Taking Tamiflu when you have first been exposed to the flu can prevent the flu from fully developing. So far, he has not run a fever.

I also called my oncologist who prescribed Tamiflu for me as well for obvious reasons. I am feeling great. Rafe has not taken it but seems to be doing well also.

My last radiation is October the 21st. I am ready to be on to the next phase which is reconstruction.

October 23, 2009 2:18 PM, CDT

I finished my last radiation treatment on Wednesday. Praise God!!! When I saw my girls at Bible Study on Monday morning, they asked if my burn from the radiation hurt. I said not too much. I spoke too soon. Those last 3 treatments burnt me to a crisp. I have a big blister under my left arm and several small ones on my chest. I am using some antimicrobial silver gel on the blisters and then Aquaphor all over. It seems to be feeling a little better today.

While I didn't get to ring a bell like they do at MD Anderson when they finish treatment, I did get a certificate signed by all of the staff at Verity Radiation Oncology. :-) I have it pinned on the wall above my desk.

My reconstruction surgery has been moved to December 15th. It had been scheduled for the 4th, but my doctor wanted me to have more time for me to recover from my radiation.

I haven't posted yet what that surgery will be like. I have opted for the lengthier procedure as it will be a permanent solution as opposed to just having implants that will most likely have to be replaced every couple of years—implants and radiation don't do well together. The procedure I am having is where they will take sections of skin and fat from my stomach, basically a tummy tuck, and use those sections to make my new breasts. I will not need any kind of an implant in this case. The downside is that this procedure takes 12 hours. And I will spend another 4 days in the hospital. It will not be easy. I am not happy about that, but I am looking at it from the positive side that once I've had this, I will be done. Plus, I will have a flat stomach once again! Without stomach crunches! Gotta love that!

October 27, 2009 7:19 PM, CDT

Discovered some good news today. I say "discovered" because I finally looked at Walker's school calendar. I thought that Walker was going to have 3 early release days the same week as my surgery (right before the Christmas break). When I looked today, I discovered that the semester doesn't actually end until mid-January, so his early release days will be then. Yeah!!! That is one less thing to worry about. However, Rafe reminded me that his students' finals *are* that week. That will make taking days off tough for him. But at least with Walker in school full days (until 3:00pm) and I believe Hope will be in school all that week as well, we won't have to worry too much about them. In fact, I have told Rafe to take off the day of my surgery, but go ahead and work on the 16th and 17th, while I am in the hospital. We will have to find after school child care for Hope until Rafe can get home, but I know my wonderful friends and family will volunteer for that. (Hint. Hint.)

I seem to have lymphedema from the removal of those two lymph nodes. My left arm has been giving me lots of trouble—extremely sore and slightly swollen. I went to see the Nurse Practitioner at my surgeon's office and she has referred me to have an eval and treatment at a Physical therapists' office. I am told the treatment is a lymphatic massage, and I will be fitted for a pressure sleeve. My appointment there is November 11th.

I have a meeting with my plastic surgeon in early November to discuss my reconstruction surgery.

I go in tomorrow to receive Herceptin. This big dose makes me feel weak and sickly. Luckily it only lasts one night.

16

November of 2009 — As my healing continued, my posts became less frequent. I began to feel better and therefore was able to do more things that took my time and attention away from the computer, and away from cancer.

November 24, 2009 7:45 PM, CST

My lymphedema continues to cause me some issues. The swelling had decreased significantly from the banding when on Saturday I developed a rash on that arm. So I have it off now, but my arm hurts when I don't wear it. I don't mind the big arm, but I would rather not have the pain. Of course, I don't want an allergic reaction either. I will see the OT again next week.

I had bloodwork done today for my surgery. My surgery is still scheduled for December 15th. I also have to turn in a ton of paperwork and get my prescriptions filled. On the day of the surgery, I have to be there by 5:30 am. It's a good thing I will be asleep most of that day! Poor Rafe though!

17

*December of 2009 was reconstruction surgery month!
It was a 13 hour surgery and a long recovery time,
both in and out of the hospital.*

December 7, 2009 8:15 PM, CST

Hi friends and family! I hope you all had a wonderful and relaxing Thanksgiving holiday! We had a very nice but short visit with Rafe's mom, dad, sister, brothers, and spouses and kids while in Corpus Christi with only minor hiccups, and Hope and I got a nice but short visit with my parents and sisters, et al., in Round Rock the day before Thanksgiving.

My reconstruction surgery is next Tuesday, December 15th. The surgery starts at 7:30 which means I have to be at the hospital by 5:30. Yikes!! My mom has already offered to spend the night here at our house on Monday night so that Rafe can take me on to the hospital while she gets the kids off to school.

Walker's attendant, Ms. Tonja, will be here for Walker every day after school. And a few angels have volunteered to keep Hope every day after school.

Walker has a doctor's appt tomorrow (Tuesday). Then on Wednesday, I get my Herceptin. Then on

Thursday, I go back to Baylor Physical therapy for my lymphatic massage. My arm is getting better, by the way. Then on Friday, I guess Hope and I will try to go see Santa at the mall in Frisco.

Next Monday, I have one more appt with Physical therapy and then an appt to get drawn on by the plastic surgeon.

So, yes, I guess you can say, I'm busy!! Busy is good, it keeps me from worrying! Of course, it also tends to keep me from praying, and that is not good. So, if I forget, please say a prayer for me.

Last, but certainly *not* least, I got a phone call from the director at Hope's school last week. It seems that one of Santa's helpers (more like an *angel* in my book) walked into her office and paid Hope's tuition for the month of December!! What a huge blessing that is to Rafe and me!! Without me working, paying that tuition has gotten harder each month. We have just written that check with blind faith the last couple of months believing that God would find the money someplace or somehow. This month, He and his angel took care of it first. (I know you didn't want to be recognized, but I just want to say *thank you so much!*)

Love to all!!

December 14, 2009 9:55 PM, CST

Okay, here we go again! Surgery #2 is tomorrow morning. Rafe and I have to be at the hospital by 5:30. My mom is spending the night tonight so that she can put Walker on the bus and then take Hope to school at 9:00.

I am actually looking forward to a few days of rest in the hospital! :-)

The good news I received today is that I shouldn't have the issue with not being able to lift my arms up this time like I did last time. The only bad thing is because I am also having a tummy tuck, I will be stooped over for a couple of days. But at least I will be able to catch myself with my arms if I fall!

We will update this as soon as I get home which will be on Saturday.

Thanks so much for your prayers and warm wishes.

December 21, 2009 5:23 PM, CST

I am home. I am doing okay. Just tired. Also, because I must walk at about a 60 degree angle, my back hurts when I walk. My stomach hurts when I move in and out of bed and when I walk around too much. So for now I am staying in bed most of the time.

I got out of the hospital on Sunday at around noon and then went over to my mom and dad's house for that first night. I slept well that night and slept most of the morning. I was anxious to get home to my own bed and I know Walker was anxious for me to get home as well. I think he feels better just knowing I am in the house, even if he doesn't have much access to me.

I had a few scary moments at the hospital. First, during the over 12 hour surgery, I was given over 2 pints of blood. Then on my first night, my heart rate went up and my oxygen level dropped causing them to fear that I had a blood clot in my lungs. My heart rate went down quickly and my oxygen level rose just as quickly. They called in a pulmonary specialist and ordered a CT scan. They ended up canceling the CT scan after the specialist said he believed I was fine.

My heart rate jumped and my oxygen level dropped again the next night as well. They called the pulmonary specialist back in and did an xray at about 4 am. All was fine. That was the last night I had any of those issues. My God is faithful!!!

I will update more later.

December 27, 2009 5:44 PM, CST

Hi friends and family! I hope you all had a very Merry Christmas! My sincerest wish for you all is that sometime on Christmas you had a moment or two to reflect on the true meaning of Christmas and remembered exactly what Christ has done in your lives. I think about that quite a bit lately, especially in light of where we've been over the last year.

On Christmas Eve, Rafe said, "Well, we are all alive and breathing. That is something to be thankful for." You all know Rafe. He's a man of few words but those few words usually hold great depth. Anyway, to which I added, "Yes, I am here to spend another Christmas with my family. I am very thankful for that!" I don't mind telling you all that there were moments over the last year when I didn't think I would make it.

I have an appointment with the doctor tomorrow. I should have at least 3 drains removed. Thank goodness! That will leave one. I would prefer to have them all removed, but 3 is better than none.

I have been feeling stronger every day, but yesterday, I developed a strange pain in my left shoulder blade that went all the way up to the back of my head. At first, I thought I was having a stroke or something. I made Rafe bring me an aspirin, just in case. Then Tylenol. Then I took 2 Vicodin. And then 2 acid reducer tablets. I finally came to the realization that it is the muscle under my shoulder blade there on that left side. Rafe went to get the valium script filled that the doctor had given me when I left the hospital. I took one about 30 minutes ago and now feel *oh so much better*! I guess I have probably held myself in a weird position to avoid pain in my stomach and it then turned into a huge knot in the muscle in my back.

Thanks to all of you for sticking in with me over the last year. I can't fully express what your love and support has meant to me and my family!

One more thing, so many people have given us so many things over the last year to help us—either financial help, assistance with kids, meals, prayers, or even moral support. It *all* has been helpful to us!!! I haven't posted everything we've gotten, one because I'm not sure I could post it all, and two because I didn't want anyone to think we were all about getting "things." *But*, I do just want to mention that we do appreciate all of it!!

To our recent anonymous donor, thank you, thank you, thank you!! May God bless you as you have blessed us!!!

Love to all!

December 31, 2009 8:27 PM, CST

Happy New Year, Loved Ones!!! Wow! What a difference a year makes!! I can't believe that this time last year, I had *no* idea what was in store for me in 2009. I am so glad that God does *not* allow us to see what is ahead.

We did the unthinkable—we got a dog! Her name is Daisy Mae. She is a 7 month old black lab. Her owner was allergic and could not keep her any longer, so she gave her to us. She is fixed, house trained (somewhat) and crate trained. She is a very good dog, but is still quite a handful. I am exhausted!!! I am posting pictures of our new girl. Everyone is thrilled *except* the cat!!!

Love to all!

Happy New Year!!!

I forgot to post—I wore jeans and a sweater the other day and I *did not have a fat roll*, also known as a muffin top!!! I'm lovin' it!!!

18

January 2010—One year past diagnosis! That January truly began a new year and a new me!

January 9, 2010 9:28 PM, CST

Hi all,

I am healing nicely and should get the last drain out on Monday. I can't wait to take a real shower!!!

Love to all!

Tracy

In February 2010, I went back to work at my part time job. Because of the business of working, raising two kids, and trying to get back into living, I had less opportunity to post in the journal.

February 4, 2010 10:09 AM, CST

Well as you can probably tell, I am finding it harder and harder to find time to sit down and write in this journal.

I am back at work, slowly taking on more hours. I was overwhelmed on Monday, not because of my workload, but because of my home obligations. Going back to work just put all of that into the spotlight for me.

I am feeling great. Very little soreness. Some lymphedema in my left arm and in the left side of my back. Pushing on the latter with my hand helps it to drain. Otherwise, I am back to my old self. Okay, almost.

One thing that has me in a tizzy these days is how clingy Hope is to me lately. She wants my constant attention and wants to order me around like I am her plaything. Poor baby doesn't have anyone here at the house to play with her. And I know having a sick mom over the last year hasn't helped. But I am exhausted from trying to please her! And I feel really guilty that I don't get to spend as much time with Walker, because I am dealing with Hope. I had really hoped (no pun intended) that she would be better once she turned 5. But I guess, as someone reminded me yesterday, she's only been 5 for a week.

I am supposed to have a scan done sometime soon. I have finished with my year's worth of Herceptin treatments. Yeah! So my oncologist wants a "finished" scan. He told me he doesn't do scans on a yearly basis but will instead get xrays and blood work from me every 6 months for the next 5 years or so.

Daisy, the dog, is doing great. She is getting so much better about going outside willingly—except today since it is rainy and cold. She is becoming a great buddy to Walker. Walker offers immediate reinforcement to Daisy since he tends to drop food everywhere he goes. She loves it!!! The minute he gets home from school, she is by his side the entire time. And sometimes, they get to running through the house together. I know, I shouldn't let either of them do it, but it is just so cute. Sometimes Walker will be in the lead and sometimes it's Daisy. And Walker is laughing and hollering the whole way! Plus, with it being cold outside, they both need the exercise.

Just want to say thanks again to everyone who has given us love and support over the past year. A special thanks to my coworkers for holding a place for me and welcoming me back with open arms. I am soooo thankful and feel very blessed to get to work with all of you!!!

February 12, 2010 10:46 PM, CST

We had a snow day today here in Dallas. It snowed all day and night yesterday. I believe they said this is the most snow we've had since 1942.

Today it was like walking in a slushee — without the good flavors.

We had lots of fun playing in the snow. It wasn't terribly cold, so everyone was out and enjoying it. When we came home, we all had to change our clothes because we were soaking wet.

In March and April of 2010, I continued to work and enjoy my family. I also had my first post treatment and surgery CT/PET scan.

March 17, 2010 9:12 PM, CDT

Spring break is here! Oh boy!!! What does spring break mean in the McCain household? Well, it means that by Saturday, Rafe and I will be ready to go back to work!

April will be a big month for me. I will go back to see my plastic surgeon. He will check on my recovery progress and talk to me about my next surgery. *Yes*, that's right—another surgery. He has promised me that this one will only be about 2 hours long (as opposed to the 13 hours last time).

I will also have a CT or PET scan, not sure which yet, and then a follow up with my oncologist. Keep on praying my wonderful friends and family!!!

Love to you all!

19

*In May of 2010, I had another reconstruction sur-
gery. This one was short and was performed at an
outpatient surgery center in Dallas. I also received
news that my PET/CT scan was clear, meaning that
there was no evidence of cancer anywhere in my
body. In other words, I was cancer free.*

*On a very sad note, I also learned that month that
a good friend of mine would lose her battle with
cancer. She had been battling cervical cancer for over
three years. It had metastasized to her lung and then
finally her brain. She had been such an important
figure for me in my battle, even though she had a
different type of cancer than I did, and to hear that
she was not going to win her battle was scary.*

May 10, 2010 10:51 PM, CDT

I can't believe it's been so long since I've updated
this journal. Life's been busy, busy, busy!

In April, I had a PET/CT scan and I am very happy
to announce that the results were *excellent!!* Nothing
appeared out of the ordinary. I am cancer free!

I also met with my oncologist who confirmed those
results. I see him again in three months. Before I see
him again, I will need to get another echocardiogram. I also will need to have a bone scan done.

Because I've been on chemo, and because I've been pushed into menopause early, I am at a higher risk for osteoporosis.

I also met with my plastic surgeon. I have another reconstruction surgery scheduled for this Wednesday, the 12th. It will be done at the Day surgery facility and not at the hospital. Should be a piece of cake! I am looking forward to getting a few "little fixes" that have been bothering me about my appearance. It's ridiculous to be vein about such things, but I would like to look as good as possible. What can I say? I'm human!

My plastic surgeon has made me promise that I will show off his handiwork by wearing a bikini while (on vacation) in Mexico. (He said he will feel like all of his hard work was wasted if I do not.) So, I am desperately trying to lose some weight between now and then!!! Yes, my stomach is flat, but that extra weight is *not* pretty! I'll let you know how it goes, but don't expect me to post any pics of me in a bikini! That's just not gonna happen!

On a very sad note, a good friend of mine from work is losing her battle with cancer. Her name is Jamie. She was very helpful to me when I got my diagnosis and even made me a care package of things she knew would make my battle a little easier. Several of us went to visit her in the hospital today. Her family are having to make some really tough decisions right now like whether she will stay in the hospital or to take her home and use hospice care.

Jamie is an incredible young woman who is always upbeat and positive, even through her circumstances right now. I can certainly understand why God would want her home with Him. But, His kingdom's gain is a great loss to those here on earth who know and love her. Please pray for Jamie and her husband, Ryan, and for her friends and family who are having to say goodbye to her.

Love to all!!!

May 13, 2010 1:01 PM, CDT

Surgery went well yesterday. No issues that I know of. I feel okay today but just really sore. I am taking Vicodin for the pain.

When I woke up yesterday, that had me in a black surgical bra! I think that is just fabulous!!! Great to feel a little sexy after such a procedure!

Thanks to Walker's attendant Tonja for dealing with him yesterday. Thanks to our friend Janet for picking Hope up from school and keeping her yesterday and also for the dinner. Thanks so much to my sister, for being there for me once again and for bringing me home. And thanks to my wonderful husband for taking such good care of me and the kids! Thank you to my precious Hopey for bringing me jello in bed last night. And thanks to God for always sticking with me. And thank you to all of you, my friends and family for your thoughts and prayers.

I love you all!!!

20

The summer of 2010 was busy with a variety of vacations and my very last surgery. At the end of the summer, Rafe and I went back to work and the kids went back to school. Life began again officially that month.

August 15, 2010 7:05 PM, CDT

Hi all,

I know it has been forever since I updated, but please know in this case that no news is good news.

This has been an extremely busy summer. Rafe and I went to Playa del Carmen, Mexico to celebrate our twentieth wedding anniversary while our son went to a camp for individuals with special needs.

Hope had a great time with Grandma and Grandpa and her aunts and cousins while we were gone.

When we got home, Rafe and Hope drove down to Corpus Christi for a few days to spend some time with Mimi and Pa in Corpus Christi and Hope's aunts and uncles and cousins there. I know they had a great time.

The first week of July was our trip to Joni and Friends Family Retreat. We had a super time this year as well. In fact, I think this year was Walker's best year at JAF camp. His allergies were really bothering him while we were there, but despite that, he managed to stay in a pretty good mood the entire time. And Hope had a blast as usual!

Finally, I had my very last surgery! (Everyone cheer here!) At least we hope that is the last one. I won't get into specifics, but this one was more reconstruction to make me look real. :-) It was a day surgery and was a quick and easy recovery. The worst issue I had was an allergy to the surgical glue, which I have had several times now. I had to go on steroids to deal with that.

Never have I felt more insecure about the world in which I live than I have this summer. And *never* have I been so grateful to have Jesus Christ in my life! He is my constant! Even when the world is spinning completely out of control, I know that Jesus is with me. He has His hands in my life and He won't let go. When you realize how shaky the ground is underneath our feet, the more you know that you need Jesus. And I can say, I need Him!

August 15, 2010 8:32 PM, CDT

I forgot to add that work starts back up for Rafe and me tomorrow (Monday, August 16th). Then the kids both head to school on the 23rd. In fact, Hope will be starting Kindergarten! Yippee!

With work and family, I probably won't get much of a chance to write updates here. But then again, you are all probably sick of hearing about me!

If I haven't said it before, let me say thank you to all of you who have prayed, called, sent gifts, sent money, brought toilet paper, brought meals, fixed my water heater, left messages here, and the many other things that all of you did for our family. It has meant the world to me and Rafe. We honestly could not have made it through the last year and a half without you! God bless you all!

Tracy

Tracy's first haircut by Rafe

Tracy and Hope

EPILOGUE

The year and a half represented in this journal seems like such a short period of time, but while we were going through it, it seemed like a lifetime. We were in a battle for my life and for our life together as a family. When it was over, we knew we had experienced a miracle. When I look back over it now, I am amazed at how prominent God's mighty hand was in every event, big and small.

When you go through something in your life, you want to believe there is a purpose in it. As a Christian, we are told to believe that God will turn that hardship into good for those who love him. The year and half of my cancer treatment, I not only believed it but mistakenly felt that the purpose would be clear to me at the end. Unfortunately that was not the case. In fact, it was all very anticlimactic. I got well, went back to work, continued on with my duties as a wife and mom—even more so when all of the meals from friends stopped coming—and life returned as usual. My son still had autism. We still had financial woes. Life was still hard. Worse than that, I now knew that God wouldn't magically protect me from getting cancer just because of my duties as the mom of a child with autism. In fact, the stress from this life made my chances of a repeat even greater.

About six months following the end of my treatment, I had the biggest breakdown of faith that I had ever experienced, even bigger than the year when my son was diagnosed with autism. I felt distanced from God like I had never before. Finally, one night, when I couldn't sleep, I got up, went into the kitchen to have a talk with my God. My first question was, "Where are you?" He responded clearly, "I am here." I opened up to him, just like the night I had it out with him over Walker's autism diagnosis. Only this time I wasn't mad at him for allowing me to get cancer. I just wanted him to know that I was scared. "I have to believe that I can count on you Lord. What do you want from me?" Just like before, his message was loud and clear. I can count on Him. Yes, bad things may happen, but I can trust that I will never go through it alone. He will always come rushing to the rescue. Suddenly a peace that surpasses all understanding came over me, just like the Bible describes.

I often see memes on social media about how much cancer sucks. Honestly, I couldn't agree more—but I now know that through this horrible thing that had threatened to destroy my life and my family, we got to witness something that very few people ever see. We saw God coming to the rescue. We saw Him in every meal, every sack of groceries, every card, every check, every friend, every doctor, and every nurse. We saw Him in very obvious places, like our church, and some not so obvious ones, like friends of friends and even in total strangers. I saw Him in the chemo lounge, at the hospital, and in the waiting room at radiology.

At this writing, six years have passed since that terrifying diagnosis. While the fear that Rafe and I experienced that year has faded for the most part, the beauty of friendships made, love felt, prayers delivered, are still fresh in our hearts and minds. My hair is back. I've gained a few pounds. I have six years of new lines on my face, and scars on my body that signify a battle. I am thankful for all of it.

Even though I am currently fine, cancer, once defeated, can lurk in the dark, just waiting for an opportunity to take a foothold. Even though every scan I have had in the last five years has shown me free of cancer, that lurking demon is always in the back of my mind. Every ache, every new pain, can bring that fear to mind and send me spiraling to dark places emotionally and running to my oncologist physically. That is the simple fact. I am human, and I tend to allow it to get the best of me at times.

Regardless of what happens to my physical self, I know where my soul will end up. I know Who is in control. God's promise of grace is always fresh on my mind. Seeing my own mortality has forced me to focus on what God has placed in front of me today, because none of us knows what tomorrow will bring. I know that the Lord walks with me, and as long as my Lord has His hands on me, I know all is well. I am well.

Visit us at *www.qpbooks.com*.

CPSIA information can be obtained at www.ICGtesting.com
Printed in the USA
LVOW07s1820281115

464508LV00024B/1247/P